C000216035

HIGH ON...

SCANDINAVIAN ARCHITECTS

HIGH ON...

SCANDINAVIAN ARCHITECTS

CURATED BY TANJA SCHMELZER

Editorial project:
2020 © **booq** publishing, S.L.
c/ Domènech, 7-9, 2º 1ª
08012 Barcelona, Spain
T: +34 93 268 80 88
www.booqpublishing.com

ISBN 978-84-9936-697-5

Curator:
Tanja Schmelzer
© HIGH ON... by Ralf Daab

Editorial coordinator and layout:
Claudia Martínez Alonso

Art director:
Mireia Casanovas Soley

Translation:
booq publishing

Translation introduction:
Gérard A. Goodrow

Printing in Spain

booq affirms that it possesses all the necessary rights for the publication of this material and has duly paid all royalties related to the authors' and photographers' rights. **booq** also affirms that is has violated no property rights and has respected common law, all authors' rights and other rights that could be relevant. Finally, **booq** affirms that this book contains neither obscene nor slanderous material.
The total or partial reproduction of this book without the authorization of the publishers violates the two rights reserved; any use must be requested in advance.
In some cases it might have been impossible to locate copyright owners of the images published in this book. Please contact the publisher if you are the copyright owner in such a case.

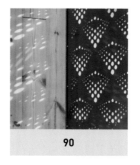

150

NORDIC — OFFICE OF
ARCHITECTURE

160

PES-ARCHITECTS

170

RJ ARKITEKTUR

180

ROTSTEIN ARKITEKTER

190

SANAKSENAHO ARCHITECTS

200

SCHAUMAN & NORDGREN
ARCHITECTS

210

SNORRE STINESSEN
ARCHITECTURE

220

TEGNESTUEN LOKAL

230

THG ARCHITECTS

240

TRIGUEIROS ARCHITECTURE

250

TUOMO SIITONEN ARCHITECTS

260

VARIOUS ARCHITECTS

270

YRKI ARCHITECTS

280

ZEPPELIN ARKITEKTAR

290
DIRECTORY

Twenty-eight SCANDINAVIAN ARCHITECTS from five countries present their works here; works that create social, ecological, economic, and emotional added value.

Whether large or small, sharp-edged or soft, coarse or fine: The architecture depicted in this volume is carried by the individual flair of Scandinavia, which is made literally palpable through the sense of free spirit and respect for people and the environment and lends a special quality of life. The presented projects from the areas of residential, commercial, and public buildings represent here an excerpt of the manifold possibilities for new living spaces, which the architects from Denmark, Sweden, Norway, Finland, and Iceland have developed flexibly and individually in cooperation with their clients. In harmony with sustainability, daring ideas were courageously implemented, subtle details were patiently shaped, complicated tasks were intelligently solved, and places for meeting and retreat were sensitively built.

Insight into the Scandinavian notion of creative design and aesthetic reflection with the built space is impressively opened by the generosity of the architects presented in this volume.

Tanja Schmelzer

ALT ARCHITECTS

Tuomas Niemelä, Anni Saviaro, Kalle Vahtera, Tanya Yliaho,
Hanna-Kaisa Karppinen, Anniina Valjus, Jyri Fält, Antti Karsikas,
Hanna-Maija Tervo, Ville-Pekka Ikola

Alt architects are based in Northern Finland. We design schools, kindergartens and other public buildings for local communities. We strive to create high-end sustainable architecture that is reasonable and flawlessly functional. We have a strong commitment to context in our design work. Solutions emerge from analyzing the site and the given brief. We appreciate the character of the low, flat northern light and natural materials that are in harmony with their environment and us humans. Resources must be used wisely and sparingly. We believe that we should only build things that lift the human spirit. Thus, whatever we make must be beautiful and inspirational to be lasting. We believe in leaving everything a little better than it was.

OULU I FINLAND

LEHTIKANGAS MULTIFUNCTIONAL BUILDING

The architecture is derived from interplay of two halves divided by a meandering gorge-like void. Lehtikangas multifunctional building comprises of a school, a regional library and a kindergarten. The new building replaces a school that previously stood on the site and combines many public functions of the area. An inviting canyon built with grey brick transforms into a functional core of the building – a common restaurant space. Located near the entrance, the library supports autonomous information gathering. Visitors are also welcome into the public parts of the building. One side of the gorge consists of the school. The other side is formed by the kindergarten, auxiliary spaces and physical education facilities. Combining different educational units into an open, transformable and cell-like structures allows students and staff to communicate and exchange ideas freely, and the students can be taught in varying assemblies. Light-coloured walls with glazing and birch detailing create the serene background needed for daily activities.

TUUPALA ELEMENTARY SCHOOL

Tuupala Elementary School is the first CLT-constructed school building in Finland. It is located in the small town of Kuhmo, near the Russian border. The school is truly a local building: the main building material, wood, is cut from local forests, while the CLT-factory and wood mill are only a few kilometers from the site. The large building mass is divided in three parts and further arranged in a village-like composition. Building volumes are complemented by smaller scaled canopies that mediate between the school yard and the building. The CLT structure can be read from the facades: where there is timber cladding, there is a CLT element. The interior architecture is strongly based on visible wooden surfaces: CLT and plywood. The atmosphere inside the building is serene. The goal was to create simple spaces where the users – children – bring colour and action to play. Tuupala Elementary School was awarded the Finnish Wood Price and shortlisted for the Finlandia Price for Architecture in 2018. The building has been widely published in magazines, books and blogs.

TEACHER'S DEN / VUORIKATU 2

This addition replaces a damaged wing of an educational building with new offices and a breakroom for teachers. A massive wooden structure was used as a pilot project in Kajaani. We chose CLT because of the resulting simple structural system that has many benefits for the users when left exposed on the inside. Produced locally from rapidly renewing forests, the structure serves as a carbon sink for the lifespan of the building. The building consists of activity-based office spaces with quiet corners and a cozy lounge for breaks. The design of the roof line and extensive glazing give the small public building a distinct profile. The interior courtyard has a more regular facade that connects the extension to the existing building. The facade is flame retardant Siberian larch and recyclable aluminium sheeting for a durable exterior coating.

ARCASA ARCHITECTS

Per Erik Martinussen, Per Einar Knutsen, Frode Smørdal,
Torill Solberg Wikstrøm, Anne Cathrine Lund,
Eivind Bing, Karsten Hammer Hansen

Arcasa Architects vision is to provide innovative high-quality design solutions that respond to emerging sustainable design and creative solutions to suit the individual prerequisites inherent in each scheme. Our design ethos is to create spaces for living and working that meet the needs of its users and imparts flexibility as well as adaptability in the future. Arcasa boasts a true commitment to preserving and heightening essential values of your everyday life from individual dwellings to larger mixed-use schemes and commercial spaces. Our fundamental focus is to create healthy built environments both at work and at home that responds to the natural environment, the identity of the area and the public realm. Good design brings people together and as a practice we place paramount importance in the spaces we spend most of our time "where we live and work". To Arcasa – bringing meaning to these spaces is what makes our jobs worthwhile.

KVÆRNERDAMMEN

Kværnerdammen is a residential project with different tenures and types imbedded in an area with rich industrial heritage from mills, to the production of wrought iron and foundry products in the 19th century. The existing site encompasses a remaining 19th century industrial building which has been tastefully refurbished to accommodate townhouses. This is complemented by the addition of a new residential block and landscaped courtyards decorated with sensitive materials harmonizing with the character of the site. The residential scheme contains efficiently designed apartments in addition to luxury apartments. Each unit has access to an abundance of green and natural spaces with opportunities for play for different age groups and seating in the main courtyard complemented by biodiverse landscapes. The roof terrace provides a social hub for the development encouraging social interaction among residents with views towards the city centre of Oslo. The project focuses on the reintroduction and rehabilitation of industrial features through large window expanses, a wrought iron look and feel and distinct material insertions whilst responding to prerequisites such as active frontages and stepping of building mass, to provide a scheme that respects the architectural identity of the area.

EUFEMIAS HAGE

Eufemias Hage (garden) is a residential project located in Bjørvika, Oslo. The historical site became the foundation to the establishment of Oslo in the middle ages, being located by the old waterfront and the center of the city's first development. The area has been undergoing urban redevelopment, being transformed into the new cultural and urban center in Oslo. The building form of Eufemias Hage is horseshoe shaped, allowing light to spill into the main courtyard to the southwest. Balconies are situated away from the more heavily trafficked areas overlooking the courtyard. The main street facade is broken up into three bands of materials. The double height glass facade at street level connects the footfall to retail and commercial uses, the more robust grey aluminum curtain walling system with glass inserts provides privacy, views and variation in the facade, whilst the inner courtyard area and penthouse suites are wrapped in a white tone responding to the material palette in the wider context. The courtyard facade effectively uses a mix of robust light colour tones and glass to give the feeling of openness. The mixed-use scheme yields a mixture of one- and two-bedroom apartments and more luxurious penthouse suites set back from the main building line with views across the Barcode, the city and the picturesque Oslo fjord. The large communal rooftop terrace is designed to meet the needs of the users, be functional for all, as well as providing a space that promotes social integration, biodiversity and health and wellbeing. Features such as outdoor playground area, urban farming, bbq areas, sun loungers, divided lounge areas and sophisticated landscaping provides spaces that reflect a more social and flexible way of outdoor living. Eufemias Hage was the first project to achieve BREEAM-NOR Very Good in the construction phase. The project therefore became the pilot project for the development of the residential BREEAM-manual in Norway.

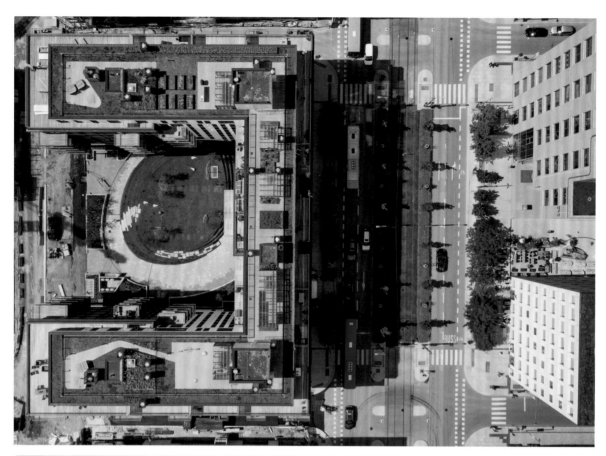

HOLMEN YACHTVÆRFT

Holmen Yachtværft is a townhouse development located near the waterfront in Nesbukta just outside of Oslo. The development hub is centered around a pedestrianised street comprising of green strips, play spaces, and seating areas. This design methodology has brought the street to the forefront imparting natural surveillance and social integration among residents through the shared amenity and varied family friendly zones. The townhouses are clad in natural and grey colored timber in staggered extruded box forms, providing relief to the periphery of the streetscape. The dwellings are three stories with a materiality that provides a strong sense of identity but responds to the local materials in the surrounding area. Each dwelling is afforded with an outdoor storage shed, entry level on the lower level, parking in the basement and large habitable spaces. The floor plans size and layout allows for flexibility giving the resident the opportunity to change the use of rooms dependent on the needs of the user. On the upper level the roof terrace provides a flexible space for outdoor living, benefitting from good sun conditions with views towards the fjord.

ARK-TELLUS

Eivind Hanch-Hansen, Sverre Aaker Sondresen

Ark-Tellus was established in 2011 by Eivind Hanch-Hansen and Sverre Aaker Sondresen. The studio is located in Tønsberg, southwest of Oslo. Architects have broad experience with housing projects of all sizes. The work of the studio is based on a tectonic discussion of construction, materials and human scale, clarified from each particular site´s topography and natural character. The dialogue between landscape and built environment and the desire to create a modern interpretation of local architecture, are consistent values.

CABIN RISØR

The summer cabin is located on a small island close to Risør on the south-eastern coast of Norway. An old cottage was sited at the island´s mid-point. The client asked for a new cabin as replacement for the old one. The new cabin is placed in the same mid-point with an outdoor atrium as a nave for all activities. All rooms are directly connected to the atrium. The building wraps around the atrium thus giving shelter for outdoor meals and calm activities. The rooms have selected views to the surrounding sea, fjord and close nature with smooth cliffs and pinetrees. The living rooms and kitchen also meet the cliffs outside on a lower level that opens towards the sea in northwest, evening sun and sunset. A colonnade along the front has specially designed moveable screens that protects the indoor spaces from the hot evening sun and gives a semi-transparent play of light and shadow to the rooms.

VILLA ROSANES

The villa is a complete remodelling of a residence from the 1920s. It was originally a Jugend-style villa, but has since been refurbished several times. With larger construction-parts damaged, a major reconstruction was required. The client asked for reconstruction which would relate to the environment consisting of classic villas, but with a contemporary interpretation. The new design preserves the main structure and retains the place on site with it´s characteristic volume and profile. The entrance, ground plan and interior has been relocated and the upper attic removed, so that the first floor has got spacious rooms underneath the pitched roof. The whole exterior of the building is clad in cedarwood and given precise detailing. Important achievements of the design has been to open up and strengthen the contact between outside and inside spaces, and provide a good flow between the different living rooms.

FAMILY HOUSE EKELUNDEN

The house is situated in the characteristic landscape of Tjøme, an island by the Oslofjord. The small existing farmhouse dates from 1870 and is well preserved. The client asked for an extension twice the size of the original 50 square metre house. The client and the architects found a common passion for nature and landscaping. The site is located in a lush broad-leaved forest with characteristic smooth cliffs which raise from the forest floor like the back of a whale breaking the waves. The architects recognised the challenge of new expressions meeting the vernacular, and maintaining strong characters in mutual respect. The two now rest solemnly next to each other and gently connect. The house has adopted an oaktree from the forest within it´s atrium. A play evolves as all the rooms surround the atrium and take part in the landscape, the forest and the ever changing seasons.

ARKITEKT MANUELA HARDY

Manuela Hardy

The half Swiss- half Norwegian architect started her own company late in 2017. She also has a background in interior design, and is keen on creating holistic architecture, working inside out, or outside in. Mainly working in the segment of detached houses and cottages, she always works closely together with her clients to achieve the best possible results. Another main method in her work, is to have an intuitive approach to every project. A well-designed home will result in feeling good for the habitants and their visitors. The outcome should always have character, function well in everyday life, as well as being unique at the same time. Therefore, it is important to treat every design process individually. Functionality, aesthetics and experience are key words in every project. The architecture should work as a backdrop or scenery, while the customer plays the main role in every home or project.

SANDNES I NORWAY

SVAL PERGOLA (THE SAA PROJECT)

The background for this pergola was to design a small sculptural ornament for the garden. The prototype be-ing built in a garden in Sandefjord, is also available as a pre-cut project for all garden-owners. Hardy has thus created a small side project that contains both a pergola and an annex. SAA (saaute.no) is the name of this project. The pergola is double-curved, and in a way inspired by the architect's crooked spine, namely scoliosis. Perfection is boring, and we may all be bent without being broken.

VILLA SOLBAKKEN

Jæren might be the most beautiful place in Norway. And at Klepp we find this plot, which has been owned by a local family for years. Now it was the family's son's turn to realize his dream home. And it just happened to be in the same area as his parents, in the garden where he grew up. The family of 5 needed a functional house with an exciting facade towards the access side, and an a more open facade towards the beautiful lakeview. Arriving from the hill a little higher than the house is situated, the roof naturally becomes a facade. The house appears to have a flat roof when viewed from the garden, but a diagonal ridge breaks the house's roof down towards the north. The roof is covered with sedum, so the house will almost appear as a part of the landscape watching it from the hill behind.

VILLA MORGENSTJERNE / MORNING STAR

This will be the home of a creative and musical family located just outside of downtown Oslo. The house is being built on a lot which was separated from the adjacent property and, although its design differs quite radically from the surrounding structures, it is well within the official regulation. The design of the project is born out of the architect's holistic, Scandinavian philosophy merged with the client's own interest in stylistic architecture and design. The inspiration behind the design, favoring light and spacious rooms, were in turn inspired by some of the Case Study Houses being built in Los Angeles, an architectural experiment extolling the virtues of modernist theory and industrial materials in the 1940s and 1960s.

VILLA BRAATHEN

This home, which is located in Porsgrunn, Norway, was originally designed in a completely different way. The first draft was not approved by the municipality, and Hardy was hired to make modifications that would result in an effective approval process. This resulted in a completely new draft on the drawing board, making the total area smaller than it originally was. The building regulations required the roof to have a certain angle, and for the house to lie nicely in the terrain, a gabled roof was chosen.

ASAS ARKITEKTUR

Ola Spangen

ASAS is a well established architecture office founded in 1980 and based in three different locations in Norway. Our field of knowledge spans from the in situ furniture to big master plans. Typical building typologies are health care buildings, housing, school, kindergartens and offices, in both private and public sectors. We consist of 19 architects, interior designers, urbanists and graphic designers in a nonhierarchical system with a social profile. We have a strong reputation as a versatile, playful and tidy architecture office. Our mantra is precision at all levels. We always promise ourselves and our clients to deliver solid and innovative projects. A variety in approaches is essential to a successful result. Ideas and concepts are brought to paper by hand as our main working tool. Hand sketching is supplied by testing spatial qualities in physical models before the projects enter the 3D digital world. This gives our team time to investigate the optimal relation between form, space and function, and to choose the correct strategy for sustainability, systems and materials. This is *valuable architecture* and the purpose of our office.

HAMAR OSLO FOSEN I NORWAY

TONEHEIM FOLKEHØGSKOLE – STUDENT HOUSING

The project contains new student housing at Toneheim Folkehøgskole in the county of Innlandet, Norway. The project is organized around a common yard, a Norwegian traditional typology called "tun", a place where traditions meets modern architecture with a personal expression. CLT is used in the buildings for the inner walls and roofs, which both reduces the building time and improves the climate inside. The external cladding is kebony, which gives the buildings a grey patina with age. Toneheim is designed according to the passive house standard with a compact plan and a chained building structure with smaller facades and thus a limited loss of heat from the building blocks. The stairwells functions as environmental towers bringing day light to the core, sends unwanted surplus heat out of the building and has sun catchers facing south, for water heating. This roof tower landscape connects to the tower at Vang church as the local context and emphasizes a vernacular architectural feature with multiple functions.

SKRIVESTUE FALDBAKKEN

The Skrivestue Faldbakken is situated in the rural areas outside the city of Hamar. The big site has a great view overlooking the fields dancing down towards Norway's largest lake Mjøsa, and consists of several linked houses from different eras. The client is the well known author Knut Faldbakken and his wife Kirvil. The new extension of the house is designed to link the different existing buildings. It is planned as a contemporary wooden building designed to emphasize outward views and the use of natural light. Old and new houses meet with mutual respect to one another, both indoors and outdoors. The function of the 20 sqm house is triple; writing room, family room and winter garden. Shapes and materiality of the box follows and respects the existing buildings, and the transitions are emphasized as recessions in the facade. The construction is made of CLT and the cladding is spruce treated with iron sulphate.

GOA ARKITEKTKONTOR

Johannes Goa Ludvigsen

GOA Arkitektkontor was founded in 2012 by Johannes Goa Ludvigsen with an ambition to create simple and straightforward architecture routed in the Scandinavian building tradition. A thorough understanding of local context is key to our approach, as we strive to create dynamic architecture rich in its dialogue with site and natural surroundings. Our work combines the use of natural materials and traditional construction techniques with a contemporary architectural language. During execution, we hone in on critical detailing within an economy of means, thereby giving our projects a minimal, delicate, precise and often subtly underplayed identity.

OSLO I NORWAY

CABIN EILEVSTØLEN

An isolated cabin retreat located in the open landscape surrounding Geilo, Norway. The project comprises two buildings: the main cabin and the guesthouse. The main cabin features a traditional program of three bedrooms and generous open-plan living space, all facing the spectacular view of the surrounding mountains. The guesthouse is compact and efficient in its planning, but is afforded a rich hierarchy of spaces despite its miniature footprint. The project reframes the traditional cabin typology within a contemporary architectural expression, while using form and volume to explore the gradation from enclosure to the open landscape. Rigorous yet simple detailing is applied throughout, giving both interior and exterior a sense of calm resolution.

PRIVATE HOUSE, KIRKEVEIEN

Three storey house situated in outer Oslo. Despite its compact plan, the design meets the client's aspirations for a single, open-plan living space occupying the entire second floor, and dramatic roof terrace affording glimpses of the Oslo fjord. The essence of the brief was to maximise natural light and a sense of generous openness without compromising the need for privacy from adjacent properties. These considerations drive the design and detailing of the external envelope - essentially a series of timber curtains - giving the building its characteristic external expression while also serving practical functions such as protection from falling.

LINJEKVARTALET, SØRUMSAND

A mixed-use building in the center of Sørumsand, a small town outside Oslo. Five storeys of apartments are placed atop a commercial base storey that occupies the entire site. The residential storeys take on an S-shaped footprint, thus enclosing two elevated courtyards while also optimising daylight both into the apartments themselves and for the surrounding buildings. The external envelope is primarily ordered around distinct, continuous bands of natural timber cladding. At each storey, the shifting position of private balconies serves to create an informal and playful composition that emphasizes the theme of seamless flow, and gives the building its characteristic external appearance.

GUDMUNDUR JONSSON ARKITEKTKONTOR

Gudmundur Jonsson

The Office Gudmundur Jonsson Arkitektkontor was established in 1987, based on winning a Nordic Competition for the Icelandic Concerthouse (never built). Soon after, as well winning a Competition about Library extension in Akureyri, Iceland. Gudmundur Jonsson Arkitektkontor has merit of 37 different prizes in Norwegian, Icelandic and Nordic Competitions, some of them 1st. and 2nd. prizes in important competitions. The Office has had a broad spectrum of assignments, including Cultural buildings, Cultural Exhibitions, Residences and modern Cabins. Educated by Sverre Fehn amongst other distinguished professors at Oslo School of Architecture, the Nature has influenced the works. The essence of «reading the site» has been of utmost importance, the emphasis of the dialog between nature and the house. Construction and materiality is supposed to clarify the concept, and the heritage of Functionalism is often an inspiration in the projects. Definition of volumes are often made more distinctive by the cantilevered roofs and balconies, simultaneously defining the spaces and giving excitement and dialog between the building and the landscape. An extensive use of glass is strengthening the constructive challenges. In the interior the purpose is to make surfaces appear as a softening unity, integrating closets, cabinets and technical installations to obtain maximum harmony and tranquility, enforced by the colour-palette.

OSLO I NORWAY

CASA G

The concept of Casa G is based on reading and feedback to the landscape it exists on. The characteristic landscape situation and view differences distinctively in each direction. Towards south the view to the sea and islands, towards north the characteristic triangular mountain, towards east the glacier and towards west the river and canyon. Those elements are the creator of the project, the transitions between the landscape views giving the entrance from the north and the curved plan giving a vitalized focus towards the seaside in south. When turning back the north view towards the mountain is as well enhanced with the widening view due to the fan-shape of the tilting wooden wall, being a mediator between the northern and southern landscape characteristic. The tilting is an answer and an interpretation of the glacier towards east, they are communicating and the only and huge window in that wall is creating "a painting" of the glacier experienced from the interior. The guest-wing of the building stretches to the canyon and the river towards west. Thus the building concept is a composition and dialogue of views and experiences of the various nature at site.

CASA MYHRER HAUGE

The concept of Casa Myhrer Hauge is a synthesis of bringing difficult landscape and regulation factors together. The factors being
a river down the valley on the s-vest side of the site, with prohibi-
tions to build closer than 100 meters, and the partly closed river/
stream, that I found important to open up, make use of, preserve
the nature, and bring the stream into the project as an important
feature. Due to those issues, and the wish to enhance the importance between the stream and the project, the garage and the
house are connected with a bridge floating over the landscape,
not touching it, but bringing it into importance and meditative
experience when entering the house. The nature will be brought
back as natural as possible, as it was initially in this Maridalen
forest, just enhancing the nature with simple means, with the
treatment of the Stream. To emphasise the dialog between the
woodland nature and the house, the back part is as well lifted
from the ground on stilts (in dialog with the tree-trunks), allowing the nature to flow through. The theme of the bridge is carried
through the house, dividing the official parts as living room and
dining room from the private rooms elevated on the second floor.
The intended division with separated volumes, creates the great
roof terrace, giving endless view over the Maridalen forest and
adjacent forrests in cascades of green ever-changing colours.

HELIN & CO ARCHITECTS

Pekka Helin

Helin & Co Architects is one of the leading architectural offices in Northern Europe, recognised for its sustainable and inspiring architecture, thoughtful design solutions and harmonious integration of buildings into the existing surroundings.

We have received 65 awards during our 45 years in business and have won 40 national and international competitions. Many of our designs are people's everyday environments: working spaces and housing. But our range of work is wide, covering urban master plans and redevelopment projects, retail and multifunctional complexes, transport buildings, civic and cultural buildings as well as private houses, villas and furniture designs. We have also designed the renovations of several important buildings and historical monuments.

HELSINKI I FINLAND

UPM BIOFORE HOUSE

Töölönlahti landowners, the City of Helsinki, and the State of-
fered the best of today's sites to successfully internationalized
large Finnish companies. UPM seized the opportunity and organized the first international architectural competition for the new
range of office blocks.

UPM set a target of cutting-edge architecture, both functionally
and aesthetically. The reasons for those aims lay in the company's long history at the heart of Finnish industrial and social development. The main spatial element of the interior is the informal atrium, which allows for closer communication and gives
the building an integral part of its identity. New and distinctive
solutions make the group work and brainstorming spaces dif-
fer from the ordinary. The potential of the site is exploited in
numerous west-facing terraces. Ecology and advanced energy
saving are represented by helical sunshades, the refined steel
mesh of which is the same material as the woven wire used in
processing paper.

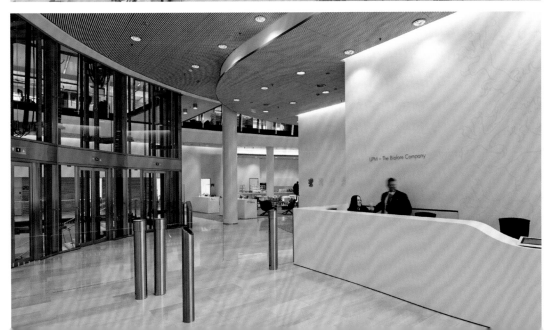

KALASATAMA HEALTH AND WELL-BEING CENTRE

Resulting from the ongoing renewal process of social and health services, Finland's health centres are currently developed into health and wellness centres based on an entirely new kind of operation model. The first new building compatible with this principle is the centre in the Kalasatama district in Helsinki. It was opened to the public in 2018. For the first time, a range of health and social services as wide as here is available under the same roof. Placed along the perimeter of the building is a client corridor spaced by waiting and self-service areas at the points of facade projections. The consulting and treatment rooms surround the building's centre area, which houses background work facilities of doctors and other specialists. These receive daylight through two large light wells as well as the high opal glass windows and top windows of the consulting rooms. The spaces of the centre were designed to be flexibly adaptable.

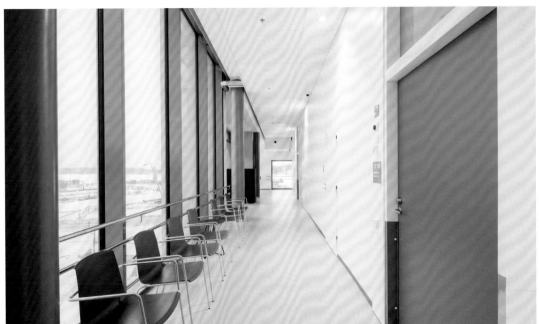

REGATTA SPA

The Regatta Spa is located on the Tehtaanniemi peninsula next to Hanko's guest harbour on a shoreline rock, which is partly in a nature reserve area. It was designed as a high-standard international bathing establishment but also to meet the Hanko citizens' needs for recreation and swimming teaching. Besides changing rooms and shower and sauna facilities, the spa contains a reception area with cafe, traditional Finnish saunas, a steam sauna, a yoga room, a gym, and several treatment rooms. In addition to the 25-metre-long main swimming pool, the equipment includes a shallower, warm therapy pool. There are also two rentable saunas and a lounge on the ground floor.

KAKA ARKITEKTER

Annika Hedeblom, Karin Skoglund

We know that great architecture makes a difference. We also know that women must step forward and take part in shaping our society and design our cities. Because of that, in 2014 we started AnniKA + KArin = KAKA Arkitekter. Through playfulness and joy, we challenge the conventional. We see the potential in each other and our projects and always encourage ideas and initiative. We approach problems and work for solutions in a committed, responsive way. Our goal is to create environments that make people feel good. We never lose sight of the whole of a project and make sure that the entirety amounts to something greater than the sum of its parts. With dedication and creativity, we realise dreams and make ideas come true. We strive to make a sustainable mark on society, today and in the future.

GÖTEBORG | SWEDEN

ÖXERYD PRE-SCHOOL

This project mixes steady and monumental with playful expressiveness. Soft materials and well-thought-out details point out that children are important. The pre-school building is situated in a forest clearing between three lakes and is intended to showcase its fine mission: to provide children with a safe, creative, and stimulating environment. The school is built with a frame of cross-laminated wood and will be certified to the highest standard. The heat-treated deal facade is completed with cedar wood shingles to accentuate the classic gable-motif. Among the references were acorns, fir cones and the surrounding woods. Inside, the cross-laminated wood is visible in the stairwell and in the studios. Wooden windows alongside half meter-high skirtings, customised shelves, benches, and a stage made of plywood adds to the nature-inspired environment. Wood and soft green notes are used throughout the building to bring the exterior into the children's spaces.

ARENA NORDSTAN

An inspiring office, leaving the visitor with more energy than when they came. That was the ambition for this co-working office Arena Nordstan, a pilot project for the property owner Vasakronan. The office is a green oasis in the middle of the shopping centre Nordstan, one of Gothenburg's busiest environments. The concept starts in the stairwell where soundscape, lighting and choice of material combine to help the visitor wind down. The project is defined by varied, colourful spaces with soft textiles and a lush greenery, providing a beautiful backdrop for the wellbeing of the tenants. Well thought-out sensory experiences and fun details stimulate movement and curiosity. Examples are twitter of birds in the greenhouse-inspired internal staircase, refreshing citrus scent in the entrance and nature-inspired sounds in the workspaces masking disturbing noise. Arena Nordstan combines a relaxed elegance with playfulness to create a workspace where personal wellbeing is central.

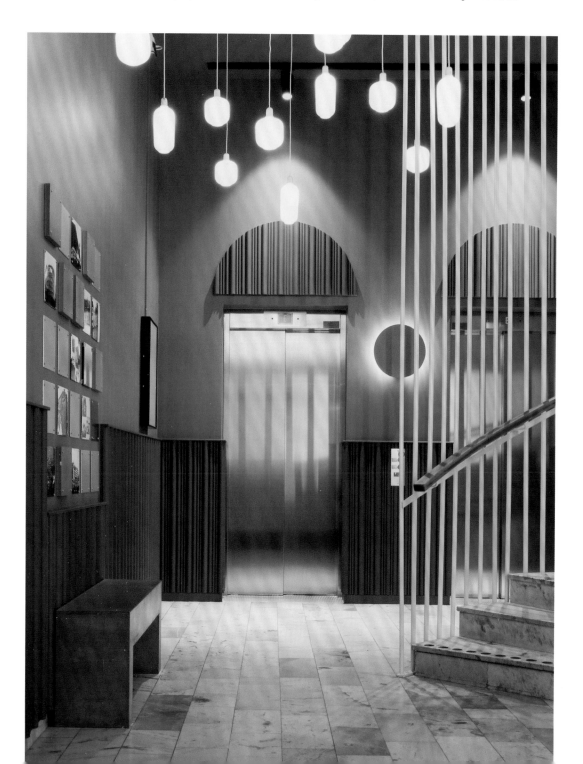

ARTILLERISTALLARNA

The Artillery Stables were built in 1835 as military riding stables. Since then they have served as workshops and a garage. Nowadays it's one of the most popular spots in the downtown area of Gothenburg. This project turned the parking garage into a coffee roasting house, bakery, furniture shop and restaurant. An architectural curator reviewed each new detail and solution before manufacturing or building. The conversion involved additional insulation, skylights, new windows in old wall openings, and a careful restauration of the surface layers to preserve and enhance the original character. A new orangery was also added. Its roof angles originate in the adjacent buildings', reassembled into a new asymmetric shape to give the extension its own identity while relating to the surroundings. Two new stairs lead to the second floor. The shape of the banisters originates in the old wall openings, multiplied into a simple and elegant steel design.

KAMINSKY ARKITEKTUR

Joakim Kaminsky

Kaminsky Arkitektur has won both the Green Dot Award and the Green Planet Award for its sustainable designs. Far too long architecture has been seen as a surface, decorations that can be added at the end of a process, instead of seeing it as a powerful tool. Therefore, we need architects like Kaminsky, architects who believe that their work can contribute to solutions to the challenges we face when it comes to climate, technological development and urbanisation. This book presents two of Kaminsky's formative projects, the Öijared hotel and Villa Bondö. These projects show that architecture, its shape and design, can be part of the solution to meet the challenges of the future as they integrate a low energy design, solar cells, local materials and wood structure in the design. The office was founded in 2007 by Fredrik Kjellgren and Joakim Kaminsky after winning the international architectural competition for the Strandbaden dance restaurant, in 2021 Fredrik left the office which is today led by Joakim Kaminsky.

GÖTEBORG | SWEDEN

VILLA BONDÖ

On the outskirts of Gothenburg, overlooking a beautiful lake surrounded by birch and pine, rests Villa Bondö, a family house with a seamless interior. Visible from the road, the facades use of larch and zinc roofing creates an anonymous appearance. The highlight of the design is the glass gable facing the lake, shielded from view as you arrive to the dwelling. Before entering the house, you can glimpse the lake through the glazed entrance but once inside you experience the breathtaking view as the building opens up to the panoramic view of the lake and the forest. The church-shaped volume of the dining hall and its structural glazing window become the centre of the interior experience. Throughout the process there was a close collaboration between the client and architect. All materials used in the house have been carefully discussed and designed to reach the vision of a minimalistic and aesthetic yet functional space for a family.

ÖIJARED

Amidst the spruce trees of the beautiful Öijared peninsula near Gothenburg, a hotel emerges. Clad in strips of timbre from the surrounding forest it seamlessly blends in with the environment. The facade is folded in six different angles to provide six unique views. The wooden slats create a play with the underlying red colour and are arranged vertically as a nod to its environment. Wooden materials used for furniture, walls, and floors are combined with textiles in warm, muted colours, inspired by the forest. The red facade is translated into a heavy curtain. The rooms are reminiscent of a walk in the deepest part of the forest. This is manifested by specially-designed dark plywood furniture, robust materials such as limestone flooring, solid oak floors, stucco-like walls in a grey dull tone, subdued green and red tones, with leather and brass fittings.

LARS GITZ ARCHITECTS

Lars Gitz

Lars Gitz Architects is a global studio for sustainable architecture, urbanism and design, founded by Lars Gitz in 1997. Since then the office has grown into an international practice with award winning work in the Scandinavian region and worldwide. Every day we create architectural quality based on innovation, experience and Nordic values. This assures sustainable and aesthetic solutions with lasting value for clients, occupants and society. We are recognised and awarded for setting new architectural standards, due to our strong focus on the functional, artistic and social value of architecture.

COPENHAGEN I DENMARK

ORIGAMI ON WATER

The Villa is designed for an art collector who lived in Asia for many years. The architecture is inspired by the clients wish to create and live in a place with a strong personal feel, embracing his interests in art and Asian philosophy. The whole concept is based on Origami, the old traditional Japanese art of paper folding from the 17th century, where the goal is to transform only a flat sheet of paper into a finished sculpture through folding and sculpting techniques. The walls and roofs are made thin and sharp to visually express the look of a single giant Origami paper, which are folded into a villa. The villa is then placed on a water reflection basin, which underlines the fragility and poetry of the Origami. The water floats inside the bearing walls and dissolves the distance between inside and outside. Towards the ocean, the water creates an infinity view, amplifying the feeling of being one with nature.

VILLA U

Based on a traditional U-shaped building, the goal is to create a more 3-dimensional architecture, where functions, surfaces and volumes are split into individual elements and then reassembled into a new composition. The individual volumes and functions appear solely as independent units, as they are part of an overall composition, which together provides a 3-dimensional overall experience of the building. The individual volumes are archetypal in their main structure, but are then added something surprisingly and irrationally, to let the poetry and the spiritual wander into the architecture. The villa is a study of how to experience the journey from the humanly defined Nordre Strandvej via ramps and stairs, and move through various clearly defined architectural spaces down to the water's own defined landscape space and horizontal plane. The facades are made in a special matt white plaster that supports the architecture, and has the ability to reflect the changing shades and colors during the day and the over the seasons. The window sections are set back in the facades to highlight the visual experience more 3-dimensionally.

VILLA JØRGENSEN

The design of the villa is based on the indisputable qualities of the plot, the view from the road and the sharp slope towards the ocean to the west. A composition of large white angled surfaces, that folds and opens with cuts in specially selected places, to close in on privacy, and open up to the view and the natural changing daylight during the day. The coverings of the villa is designed for protecting the inside against the direct sunlight during the summer months, thus allowing the sunlight to reach into the villa with light and warms during the winter months. The coverings also protect areas of the terraces from direct sunlight and provides shelters for the dew in the evening time. The villa is placed on a water reflection basin, and the water floats inside the bearing walls and dissolves the distance between inside and outside. Towards the ocean, the water creates an infinity view, amplifying the feeling of being one with nature.

VILLA GITZ

The villa is situated on Orø Island on a little peninsula, which gives a beautiful view over the ocean with the sunrise in the east, as well as over the ocean to the sunset in the west. The villa is a private summer residence, and the design is aiming to bring human as close to nature as possible, by dissolving the border between the building and the surrounding green nature and ocean. The angled walls reaches out into the landscape towards east and west, and invites the nature inside and all the way through the center main part of the villa. The nature is enhanced inside by larger trees and features the fireplace as the heart and center of the villa. The design of the fireplace is inspired by the nature as an organic contradiction to the precisely defined angled corners and walls of the villa. It rises slowly from the ground as a curved flower, and the giant leave reaches out towards east and transforms into the dining table. The dining table provides a view towards the sunrise to the east as well as a stunning view through the fireplace to the sun setting over the ocean in the evening.

The coverings of the villa is designed for protecting the inside against the direct sunlight during the summer months, thus allowing the sunlight to reach into the villa with light and warms during the winter months. The coverings also protect areas of the terraces from direct sunlight and provides shelters for the dew in the evening time. The dark warm golden facades are especially designed for the villa. They are designed as a chameleon facade in two different golden colours, which changes the colour in relation to which angle it is viewed. The facade design contributes to the unexpected and surprising elements and views, which are fluently added to invite poetry and spirituality into the architecture.

LINJA ARCHITECTS

Timo Koljonen, Ville Niskasaari, Esa Paajanen

Founded in 2006 by architects Timo Koljonen, Ville Niskasaari and Esa Paajanen, LINJA ARCHITECTS is one of the biggest architectural practices in Finland. Our offices are located in Oulu, Helsinki and Jyväskylä. With a team of 70 professionals, we operate nationwide and draw on experience from over 700 projects. Our work encompasses every aspect in the field of architectural design, with projects covering all phases of both new building and renovation design. In addition to city planning and various development plans, we also provide interior and environmental design services. Our customers range from public institutions, construction companies and businesses to private individuals. We approach every design project with an open and innovative attitude. With each commission we strive to attain a high standard of superior quality, regardless of the scope of the project at hand. We pride ourselves on selecting the appropriate design methods and tools in order to meet the exact needs of every individual assignment. Our designs have been featured in numerous professional journals in Finland and abroad, and we have also obtained several awards in architectural competitions.

HELSINKI OULU JYVÄSKYLÄ I FINLAND

MULTI-PURPOSE HOUSE MONIKKO, NURMIJÄRVI, FINLAND

Nurmijärvi is a rural municipality in the Greater Helsinki area. Managed by the youth services of municipality of Nurmijärvi, MONIKKO is a multi-purpose building offering leisure activities and hobbies, especially for children and young people. The building has spaces for art education, a leisure place for young people, changing rooms for sports and a multi-purpose event hall with capacity to seat audiences of 400 people. The multi-purpose hall offers a high-quality setting for a variety of events, ranging from pop concerts to classical music concerts as well as offering spaces for corporate and private events. The easily convertible event hall has a rising auditorium and adjustable acoustics. The auditorium can be built into an ascending mode or into a plain floor creating space for standing auditorium.

VOCATIONAL COLLEGE LIVE, ESPOO, FINLAND

Located within the lively Turuntie district of Leppävaara, Espoo, is the new Live Vocational College building maintained by the disability foundation. Invalidisäätiö is a vocational school for secondary education and a center for the development of SEN education. It accommodates spaces for 500 SEN pupils as well as 150 members of staff. The building resides in a leafy, hilly residential area, not far from the center of Leppävaara, which is currently under development . A large shopping center, Sello, is also located to the west of the site. Featuring south and west facing facades along the busy Turuntie road, the walls are clad with vertical ceramic pipes which partially obscure the windows and filter out most of the direct sunlight. This, combined with artificial lights, will assist with the daily needs of visually impaired students. A sheltered courtyard space is formed from the buildings large curves and extended facades that blend with roof's broad canopy. The courtyard's facades are clad with ecologically silicate-impregnated wood that have aged to become beautifully grey hue. A four storey central lobby greets the visitor and is the heart of the accessible building. In addition to the class room facilities, this multi-purpose building includes high-quality music training rooms, teaching kitchen, audio and dance training facilities as well as various work practice rooms. The chosen tones and materials all work to create seamless harmony between the interior and exterior materials of the building.

MAD ARKITEKTER

Trond Elverum, Kurt Singstad, Nicolai Riise

Mad was formed as an architectural studio in 1997 by Trond Elverum, Kurt Singstad and Nicolai Riise and always has the city's best interests at heart. Today Mad is a consortium with nearly 100 employees, spread across nine companies, located in Oslo, Bergen, Stavanger and Fredrikstad. Mad are innovative, challenge convention and they always strive to turn problems into opportunity and prefer controlled processes and spectacular buildings, not the inverse. They have developed a working method which guarantees quality and which involves clients in an exciting and fruitful partnership.

OSLO FREDRIKSTAD BERGEN STAVANGER I NORWAY

THE FACULTY OF LAW

Domus Juridica is a modern university building that simultaneously compliments the historical and listed buildings in the vicinity. This is the result of a dedicated focus on working with recognisable, high quality materials and a clear verticality through large brick columns. The columns are a reimagining of the classic column motif recognisable from historic university buildings and gives the building a characteristic expression, whilst also clearly marking the entrance. Behind the columns, a passage opens up into the city block. The passage's roof and glass walls have bronze anodised aluminium profiles, which together with the red brick show a kinship to the university campus. The columns, with their specially designed bricks, gradually lean outwards from the facade before receding again towards the top. The point of inversion, where the brickwork also changes direction, occurs at a different height on each column. This feature creates beautiful shadow play in the columns themselves and gives the entire building a 3 dimensionality, which is experienced most predominantly when passing along Kristian Augusts gate. The facade is bricked with red mortar, enhancing the cohesion. The atrium is the heart of Domus Juridica and functions as an informal meeting place for visitors, students and staff. The atrium draws daylight into the core of the building and provides a clear reference point around which to orientate. The staircase and glass surfaces between rooms provide visual connections, good daylight and a clear understanding of the building's activities.

MAD BUILDING

The Mad building is possibly one of the worlds thinnest apartment blocks. The housing part measures 7.8 by 90 metres, with 15 stories of high-quality urban apartments, all with daylight from at least two sides. The buildings unique design is fine-tuned to satisfy high expectations of living quality and to adhere to the special rules laid out in the planning regulations. The building fully adheres to the Barcode-concept, on a narrow and challenging site. At its narrowest the building measures just 6 metres wide! All apartments have living rooms and balconies facing south east, where the form of the adjacent building allows for direct sunlight all day. Large glass sliding doors blur the boundaries between inside and out and an outer layer of specially designed sliding elements allows residents to shield their apartment as desired, both against the sun and visibility from outside. Material use in the building is restrained with naturally oxidised, perforated aluminium giving unique light qualities and wood cladding offering a warm glow. We dare say that the apartments in the Mad Building are the city's most spectacular!

NYGAARDSPLASSEN

A once forgotten space has evolved into a new town square serving as a hub for the area. Two new buildings establish yet another urban space; a narrow pedestrian street leading to the square. The buildings are divided into smaller segments, using varying brick types, echoing the original terraces of the area. Mad has worked to reduce the scale of the buildings in order to give the effect of passing a number of buildings, whilst the narrow streets prompt people to reduce their speed, pause and look to see behind the windows they pass by. One gets the sense that the details are talking to you and the variety of brick types around the square make it difficult to discern between those buildings which are old and those which are new. There were already several brick buildings from various eras, but few probably gave a thought as to how beautiful they are, the urban reparation has helped to emphasise their individual characteristics. Old, worn neighbouring buildings have been given new value, a whole neighbourhood has been repaired. The use of high-quality materials means that these buildings will stand for hundreds of years. The locals are genuinely proud of the new Nygaardsplassen and all feel a sense of ownership towards the revived city block, giving them confidence and renewed optimism on behalf of the town of Fredrikstad. Nygaardsplassen is an archetypal project and especially innovative way of integrating city floor programming and residents, that will ensure that the streets are full of life throughout the day. The project has helped to make the centre of Fredrikstad both a safer and more attractive residential area, for the first time in 50 years people are back living in Nygaardsplassen. Nygaardsplassen recently won Cityprisen 2020 for most innovative urban design project in Norway.

MARGEN WIGOW ARKITEKTKONTOR

Cecilia Margen Wigow

Margen Wigow Arkitektkontor AB was started in 2000 and is run by Cecilia Margen Wigow architect SAR / MSA. The office specializes in new and refurbished villas and holiday homes. We are driven by job satisfaction and a genuine interest in architecture. The aim is to create environments of high architectural value based on the client's wishes, the conditions of the site and the project budget. The ambition is to follow all the stages of the project from sketch to building follow-up in order to implement the architectural ideas down to the detail level.

STOCKHOLM I SWEDEN

PRIVATE SPA

The Spa is located in the archipelago of Stockholm. The aim has been to make the house feel part of nature. The simple rectangular volume is therefore placed low between two rock slabs. The roof consists of a floating concrete slab covered with grass and the large glass surfaces have surface-mounted wooden trellis whose climbing plants dress the house in vegetation. The entrance floor has pool room with an infinity pool, jacuzzi, relax, sauna and gym. Changing rooms, massage rooms and technical areas are located in the basement. Exterior materials, glass, wood and concrete reappear on the inside but have been supplemented with floors of Swedish limestone and slate, as well as oak carpentry. The private spa is done in collaboration with AC Sundberg Arkitekter and Bahri arkitekter.

SEASIDE CABINS

The island is located at the far end of Stockholm's outer archipelago. The new buildings are built in a valley facing a sheltered bay. The wish has been to create a modern variant of the older shanty towns, which still today re main on individual islands in Stockholm. The direction of the houses and the slope of the roof follow the shape of the mountains and are covered with sedum roofs. The facades are lined with wooden panels painted with mud paint. The main building consists of a single large room where each function is divided by the different floor levels made of solid pine boards. The walls, ceilings and furnishings are made of pine plywood. On the island there is no electricity so all houses have a fireplace for heating, refrigerator and stove powered by gas, lamps of kerosene and water pumped up by hand outdoors. The Seaside Cabins are done in collaboration with architect Per Wigow.

NORDIC — OFFICE OF ARCHITECTURE

Represented by Inger Molne, Knut Hovland, Bjørn Olav Susæg, Camilla Heier Anglero, John Arne Bjerknes, Eskild Andersen, Thomas Lindgård Fagernes, Diana Cruz

Nordic is one of Norway's leading architectural practices, with offices in Oslo, Copenhagen, Reykjavik and London. Our projects range from the world's most sustainable airport, to floating saunas on remote mountain lakes. Founded in 1979, Nordic today employs 250 architects, interior architects, landscape architects, master planners and specialists. Nordic has designed a wide range of airports in Norway and abroad, including the Oslo airport and the new Istanbul airport. We are among the leading health care architects in Norway and are also currently in charge of the project for the new Governmental headquarters in Oslo. In addition to large public buildings, we design mountain destinations, housing, and sustainable masterplans in Norway and abroad. Our mission is to build a more sustainable society through exceptional architecture that transforms, inspires and enhances the environments in which we live.

OSLO I NORWAY

NANCHANG WAVES

The project is located next to the Elephant Lake Wetland Park. The design concept is to bring the natural qualities of the wetlands into the project, creating a spatial experience where the building and the landscape blend together. The design consists of three natural elements, water, earth and sky, corresponding to three functional areas: the front square, the commercial facilities and the observation tower. The main body of the building form a continuation of the landscape elements. The rooftop garden is accessible from both sides of the building, underneath which are scattered retail and commercial functions. These are linked to the rich outdoor activity space in the front plaza, bringing vitality to the community around the project. At the end of the park facing Elephant Lake Wetlands stands the viewing tower. Accessed by a double helix stair, accessing the tower becomes a 360 degree ascent offering dramatic views of the urban development and the natural landscape.

BERGEN LUFTHAVN

Originally built for 2.8 million passengers per year, the new terminal at Bergen Airport increases the capacity to 7.5 million. Cleverly constructed in modules, the building is already prepared for future expansions without sacrificing the concept. The entire depth of the terminal is visible to the traveller. This transparency, supplemented with well-designed and legible signage, makes for a pleasant way-finding experience. The arrival hall is characterised by four dominant design elements: the hanging veil of the structural glass facade, the grand steel trusses of the support structure, the delicate timber ceiling and the dramatic entrance bridges spanning over the space. The departure hall is the architectural centrepiece of the terminal. The identity of the room is defined by the expansive tiled floor and the folded timber-clad ceiling connecting the central building and the pier. The pier opens up towards the fjord and the sky – facing the journey ahead.

SAVANNEN NURSERY

When designing Savannen Nursery, we focused on down-scaling what could have been a large volume into smaller units. Scientific studies show that small children feel safer and have fewer conflicts when they are in smaller, more easily comprehensible environments. Design concept and materials have been chosen to minimise the building's carbon footprint and give the nursery a green, sustainable profile. The playground is designed for both play, reflection, and learning. There are various areas for the different age groups – closest to the building is the area for the smallest children, where the adults are always nearby. More challenging play areas, designed for the older children, are located furthest away from the building where the theme is about exploring. The building and the playground will be open for public use in the evenings and on weekends and will serve as a gathering place for the whole community.

KVITFJELL_BASECAMP

Basecamp is situated at about 800 meters above sea level in between the skiing lanes of Kvitfjell. The area is host to world cup downhill and slalom events and a popular destination for all things ski related. The local building traditions of generous sized, yet simple barns heavily influenced the design. In accordance with these this the building is asymmetrical, making it possible to add a loft while staying within the height regulations. The roof also covers the outdoor gallery walkways and the balconies, creating shelter from the weather. Raw timber is the dominant material in the project, covering nearly all surfaces. The buildings are designed to withstand the climate without the need for heavy maintenance, and the surfaces and the scent of the natural materials help project the buildings' identity.

PES-ARCHITECTS

Tuomas Silvennoinen, Pekka Salminen, Jarkko Salminen, Arttu Suomalainen

Helsinki-based PES-Architects is among the most international architecture and interior design firms in Finland. Founded in 1968, we now have a multinational staff of over 70 and a Shanghai studio established in 2010. We work towards an architecture that embraces a cross-disciplinary approach, often engaging external designers and specialists. Our projects encompass complex and wide-ranging building types, including airports and transport terminals, performance venues, sports facilities, arenas and mixed-used developments, as well as demanding refurbishment projects. We believe that a relatively small Nordic architecture office can succeed globally provided that certain basic credentials are fulfilled: the right references, the latest technologies and an innovative team. To this we add a creative vision distinct from the international mainstream as well as a deep understanding of user experience, sound building practices and a comprehensive approach to project management.

FUZHOU STRAIT CULTURE AND ART CENTRE

The Fuzhou Strait Culture and Art Centre, completed in 2018, was the winning entry in an international invited competition in 2014. An opera house, concert hall, multi-functional theatre, exhibition hall and cinema centre are located in five petal-shaped buildings with a total area of 153,000 m². Dividing the large complex into smaller units creates human-scale spaces both inside and outdoors. The venues are linked by a cultural concourse and large roof terrace that open towards the central garden and Minjiang River. Ceramic was used throughout the complex as a functionally and aesthetically appropriate material with local historical significance. The main facades are of ceramic louvres angled to provide optimal shading. The artistic ceramic tile cladding of the opera and concert hall interiors was designed together with Taiwanese ceramic artist Samuel Hsuan-yu Shih according to exacting acoustic demands. Another Chinese material, bamboo, is also used widely for walls, flooring and detailing.

ICON YUNDUAN TOWER

Icon Yunduan Tower is a 192-metre-high mixed-use building located in a high-tech zone on the outskirts of Chengdu, China. Completed in 2018, the building is a prominent local landmark. The 47-storey complex contains commercial, hospitality and conference premises as well as offices. The main tenant is the Business & Innovation Centre for China-Europe Cooperation (CCEC). The tower has an L-shaped plan at ground level that grows into a square towards the top, forming a sweeping facade overlooking Tianfu River and a straight edge along Tianfu Avenue. The curved elevations to the south and east are defined by green terraces up to the 30th floor, while solid glass and glazed ceramic panels alternate to form a chequered pattern on the other facades. The spatial highlight of the building is the 30-metre high lobby that opens towards the river. The adjacent, partly underground concert hall was designed by local partner CSWADI.

WEST TERMINAL 2, PORT OF HELSINKI

West Terminal 2 was completed in 2017 to meet the needs of growing ferry traffic from Helsinki West Harbour on the busy Helsinki-Tallinn route. The guiding design principle was to ensure the smooth, fast and safe flow of passengers on and off ships. The terminal is compact at ground level, with a wide departure lounge raised 10 metres off the ground and placed crosswise between two berths. This allows boarding vehicle traffic to flow under the building while minimising foot passengers' walking distances between the terminal and ships. The timber ceiling of the hangar-like lounge swoops down from a height of 9 metres, directing passengers to the boarding bridges at the sides. A curved glass wall opens to a magnificent view of the sea. The sculptural form of the building evokes a giant ray or other sea creature washed ashore, with glass, concrete and aluminium facades that gleam in the sun.

RJ ARKITEKTUR

Rasmus Jørgensen

RJ Arkitektur has worked with a wide range of architectonic genres and styles from its base in Skagen since 2016. Based on the philosophy that good architecture must be accessible to every layer of society, owner Rasmus Jørgensen offers everything from upgrading of classic buildings worthy of preservation, to ultramodern, high-tech homes. This takes place in collaboration with competitive contractors in which we have full confidence. RJ Arkitektur has a close-knit network of selected specialists and a wide-ranging portfolio of clients and projects that cover everything from small private annexes to hotel properties and institutions. Through honest and creative consultancy, they bring appreciation to the scope of the project, thus resulting in rewarding architecture for the benefit of the user. At RJ Arkitektur, the psychology and experience of the building and of the individual rooms are the primary instruments, whilst great respect for surrounding environment is maintained at all times.

LUXURIOUS VILLA WITH DENMARK'S BEST VIEW

Right from the start, this building has had to strike a balance between a difficult district plan and an even more difficult plot of land. The building is built in three levels in order to meet the requirements of the district plan. The levels are pulled in to reduce the height and distance to the boundary. A derived effect of this is that it also enables the rooms at the extremes of the building to have a view of the water.

The building's somewhat hard expression is softened through the use of wood and patinated noble metals. The floor structure at first floor is executed in hardwood on all sides, which cuts through the building. The building's angled walls are executed in contrast material and cut vertically through the floor structure and "living space". This binds together the building's variety of angles and provides a holistic and integrated experience.

CONVERSION OF TYPICAL SINGLE-FAMILY HOME

The single-family home was originally built with red bricks and corrugated fibre-cement roof, and has now been updated with a facade in weather-resistant wood, black plaster and an interlocking metal roof. In order to create a modern expression with full-height windows in the "living space" and to retain existing constructions, the house was designed as two buildings with adapted styles, but with diverse window heights and expressions. In the interior, the mode of expression of the design is adapted to the architecture. The lines in terms of the layout of the rooms have been moved in order to provide a soft and seductive transition between the rooms. The central element is the wood-burning stove, which is visible from the kitchen, dining area and living room. The hard and light expressions of the design are balanced through the use of wood and dark colours, in addition to soft textiles and furnishings.

COMPLETE RESTORATION OF SKAGEN-STYLE HOUSE

The building had previously enjoyed an existence as a grocer's and residential dwelling. Over the years, it had been refurbished to varying degrees, leaving the building with a patchwork of different levels and materials. This latest refurbishment was designed to update the house with particular regard to construction quality and insulating properties, while creating a more modern expression for the interior of this classic Skagen-style house. The cabinets are a matt green hue to complement the pale, solid wooden floor and provide a comfortable and modern contrast. Existing beams, wooden ceilings and tie beams have been carefully restored, and from the "living space" two double-leafed doors were created facing out onto the patio. The first floor is utilised in full by adding dormers, whilst the surrounding patio was brought up to date in order to complete the holistic expression.

MODERN AND MINIMALIST SUMMER COTTAGE

On arrival at the house, you are met by two minimalist – though impressive – columns in an otherwise small and relatively closed facade, hiding what awaits inside. On entering the house, the walking area and the entire "living space" open up to the natural surroundings, drawing the outdoor space into the house and, in turn, the house out towards the surroundings. Walls and fixtures are executed in the same recurring materials both inside and outside, thus providing a fluid and enticing experience while drawing you towards the outdoor space. The columns from the front of the house continue to the rear and provide a more dynamic and balanced expression with a clear definition and framing of the dimensions of the building.

ROTSTEIN ARKITEKTER

Rickard Rotstein

Rotstein Arkitekter was founded in 1992 by Rickard Rotstein and is devoted to sustainable contemporary architecture. The design method is based on a careful analysis of the conditions and of the site, where the unique components of the location and its characteristics are integrated into the program of the project. The first sketches seek to achieve simplicity and clarity of the concept, the goal being to combine the basic facts into an integrated solution with a high level of authenticity, integrity and responsibility. A holistic understanding of the situation and the ability to find smart solutions provide quality, meet set requirements and create the best result. Through strong architectural ideas we create complete solutions and add new values.

STOCKHOLM I SWEDEN

SEB BANK, STOCKHOLM

Photographs of a wing of the SEB-bank (now reconstructed) in the downtown Stockholm.

BRUDERHILFE INSURANCE, KASSEL

A series of buildings connect and unite different parts of he offices of an insurance company in a city block. The facade of the building facing the street incorporates stucco and stone, and several lighter units with glass and metal are placed inside the block. Various small outdoor spaces are created between different parts of the complex with a uniquely designed landscaping, while the interiors of the offices are arranged in a half-open space layout to promote good internal communication.

LILJEHOLMSKAJEN, STOCKHOLM

The project consists of two residential blocks with a spectacular seaview and facing the new main square in the neighborhood. The facades of the two blocks create a front toward the public space, visible from a distance, and they have an associated composition with the same components of an irregular window setting, scattered balconies and intermittent outdoor rooms in glass. The window setting provides both an efficient plan layout and a pleasant variety. A kindergarten with tailored interiors is located in one of the blocks. The high fully-glazed ground floor contains restaurants and shops, opening onto terraces on the square during the summer months. Both blocks have dark grey plaster facades facing the square and a warm yellow colour on the inside.

CLIFF HOUSE, STOCKHOLM ARCHIPELAGO

This holiday home is located on a cliff in the Stockholm archipelago among rocks and pines with a magnificent seaview, and is adjacent to an undeveloped and protected nature area.

The design of the house springs from the existing topography, and the house was built on the site without the use of any large construction machinery. No rock blasting was carried out, and all the valuable trees and natural character of the land have been preserved.

SANAKSENAHO ARCHITECTS

Matti Sanaksenaho, Pirjo Sanaksenaho

Sanaksenaho Architects was founded in 1991 in Helsinki. The partners are Matti Sanaksenaho and Pirjo Sanaksenaho, who both graduated as Masters of architecture in 1993 at Helsinki University of Technology. Matti Sanaksenaho has been professor of contemporary architecture at Oulu University since 2011 and Pirjo Sanaksenaho has been professor of building design at Aalto University since 2014 and head of department of architecture since September 2019. The approach to design is closely affiliated with the visual arts, particularly minimalist sculpture. The inspiration is often drawn from nature in its various forms. These ideas are transformed into volumes, masses, spatial programs, polished forms and architectural entities. Natural, homogeneous materials with a long history of human use, such as wood, brick, concrete, steel and copper, all of which acquire an attractive patina over time. Sanaksenaho Architects strives to create architecture that captures the imagination and speaks to people on an emotional level. User-centered communication often steers their design process towards unexpected results. The office is a family-sized team, in which each member brings their own particular views and ideas to every design task. Although the vocabulary is contemporary, the effort is for a timeless result that will still be fresh and engaging in a hundred years' time. The key works include the Finnish Pavilion for the Seville World Expo in 1992, co-designed by Matti Sanaksenaho as a member of the Monark group. Other important works are St Henry's Ecumenical Art Chapel in Turku completed in 2005, Student Health Care Centre in Helsinki 2010, Villa CIPEA in Nanjing China 2012 and several private villas, one of which is House K in Espoo 2014.

HELSINKI | FINLAND

CIPEA VILLA #20 / BOAT HOUSE - NANJING, CHINA

The villa is part of CIPEA, China International Practical Exhibition of Architecture, later called as Nanjing Sifang Art Park. It takes place in Pearl Spring Tourist and Holiday Resort Zone. There is a lake in the middle of the exhibition area. Green hills and springs surround the lake. The villa is a holiday-residence. It can also serve artists in their short-term stay for art creation, family and small group tour, meetings, seminars and short-term work. The role of the building is to emphasize existing natural surroundings. The building is mostly hidden in the green forest. The villa is reflected from the surface of the water. Most public functions are situated on the entrance level. The conference room can be connected to the dining hall by opening a sliding wall. Living room opens to the lagoon with the window wall. Bedrooms are situated one floor down from the entrance level. The suite can be also an atelier for visiting artists. Two-storey suite/atelier is situated on the lowest level. The outdoor living is happening on a roof terrace. The villa is boarded with green copper. Inside surfaces are local wood. Local natural stone covers the elevator tower, the fireplace and the roof terrace. The aim of the villa is to create harmonious living in the nature. The villa might be seen also as a boat left to the shoreline.

HOUSE K

House K has been designed for a young four-person family in Saunalahti, Espoo. This particular area of low-rise housing has been densely planned. The plots are on a rocky hill along a horseshoe-shaped road. From the upper floors of the houses -there is a view all the way to the sea, unless an adjacent building happens to block it. The closeness of the neighbouring houses was the key factor in the design solution. The idea was to open up the house inwards, towards a triangular-shaped patio and further towards a larger park area so that the views from the living spaces could be made private and peaceful. The residents wished for a simple and stylish home. White-rendered concrete block walls demarcate the living room, kitchen and dining space within the main section and the sauna department in the smaller annexe. Entry into the house is given a feeling of openness by the transparency leading from the entrance hall to the terrace and upstairs. The floor surfaces downstairs are polished concrete and upstairs wide wooden floor planks. The stairs is lit by a skylight and the wooden steps are hung with steel rods from the ceiling construction. The top-lit bathroom turns a shower into a meditative experience. A wooden bridge links together the wings of the building. The bay window in the bedroom offers a place of reflection overlooking a forested landscape.

ST. HENRY'S ECUMENICAL ART CHAPEL - TURKU, FINLAND

In the landscape of the island of Hirvensalo, forested hills rise from the flat fields. The chapel is aligned east-west atop one of the hills. Its siting focuses the landscape. The green patina of the copper facades will be in harmony with the trees. The form of the chapel speaks quietly more as art. The intention is to create a large landscape sculpture and small building. The path to the chapel rises up the hill. The entrance to the chapel is through a small foyer. The foyer leads to the large hall, the stomach of the fish. The gallery and the chapel are one space. The gallery is to the rear of the space and the chapel to the front. In the event of larger ceremonies the entire space can be utilised by the addition of benches within the gallery area. Vice versa, the removal of the chapel benches allows the entire hall to be used as a gallery. The wooden altar is at the end of the axis. The interior is of wood. The contrasting play of light and shadow powerfully articulates the interior of the space. Strong indirect light enters from both ends of the chapel. The altar window is sculpted glass, created by artist Hannu Konola.

STUDENTS' HEALTH CENTRE - HELSINKI

The building for students' health care organization YTHS is based on an invited architectural competition in 2007. Sanaksenaho Architects won the competition with an entry called "Serpens". Simple elevations reflect the neighboring neo-classical Töölö quartiers in Helsinki. The health center is an extension to a previous building of YTHS built in 1970's. Between the red brick new part and the old building there is glazed inner courtyard with restaurant and entrance lobby. Doctors' rooms are on the street side and waiting areas along the curved inner brick wall. Glazed bridges connect the extension to the old part of the building. The health center was completed in 2010 and got a glass prize of the year. Sanaksenaho Architects is now designing another students' health center to Tampere.

SCHAUMAN & NORDGREN ARCHITECTS

Ted Schauman, Jonas Nordgren

Schauman & Nordgren Architects champions environments where life can flourish. Since Ted Schauman and Jonas Nordgren founded SNA in 2016, the Copenhagen- and Helsinki-based architecture and urban planning studio has practiced design that reflects and enhances the experience of communities, and which creates a sense of ownership among multiple stakeholders.

Through techniques that range from urban analysis to architectural theory, SNA commences a project by identifying challenges and potentials for diverse interest groups. The studio then seeks out these stakeholders as creative partners, inviting open dialogue as a source of innovation and long-term emotional investment. Their clients share a vision of collaborative process as the means of unlocking value within the fields of architecture, landscape design, and planning. Together, they make places where inclusion and well-being may be felt for generations.

COPENHAGEN I DENMARK   HELSINKI I FINLAND

VILLA FAVRE

Villa Favre is a two-family house located in Le Mont-sur-Lausanne, Switzerland, a northern district of Lausanne on Lake Geneva. The house comprises a 200-square-meter residence for the Favre family, as well as a 100-square-meter unit that is rented out long-term. SNA made these allocations legible in the footprint of the house, which assumes an irregular hexagonal shape. The decision creates privacy for the two families, in turn. Separate entrances face away from one another, and differently angled windows prevent looking into the adjoining yard.

The facade further expresses a two-part interior configuration. The ground floors of both residences are public areas for eating, working, and socializing, whereas the upper floors are meant for rest and relaxation. Shutters fitted to the upstairs windows can be closed for the night, like a metaphor: the building closes its eyes when it goes to sleep. Exterior materials further illustrate the floors' different functions, and SNA's banding of striated concrete and wood evokes the wooded location. A generous roof terrace with garden tops the composition, where the Favre family can reside and get stunning views of the gentle hillside site and the wider surroundings. In collaboration with Meyer Architects.

The SNA team: Ted Schauman, Jonas Nordgren, Kristian Kontula, David Monteiro. Photo credits, Nicolas Sedlatchek.

MOLLIS

A visually lightweight and human-scaled chair, Mollis is a low-slung seat for reclining and easy conversation. The slender wooden seat is fabricated from moulded veneer that curves around the body; the ergonomic shape is made more comfortable by a foam seat pad upholstered in fabric or leather, and it is cradled by a double-cross steel leg frame. Although it appears remarkably minimalistic, Mollis is rife with historical references. The steel frame evokes the hairpin legs of 1950s-era furniture design, while the frame references Charles and Ray Eames' experiments with moulded veneer. The overall geometry of the chair also harkens to Arne Jacobsen and even the ancient Greeks, who developed the elegant klismos form. In all, Mollis establishes a dialogue with multiple precedents without sacrificing its own, innovative identity.

Prior to cofounding SNA with Ted Schauman, Jonas Nordgren was named one of the world's foremost contemporary furniture designers by *Wallpaper* magazine. The easy chair was developed together with Artur Moustafa for VUJJ, later RVW. Photo credits, Ludvig Holtenäs and Mikael Dahl.

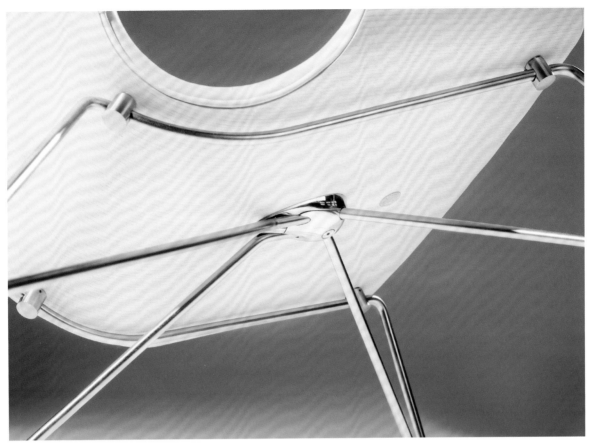

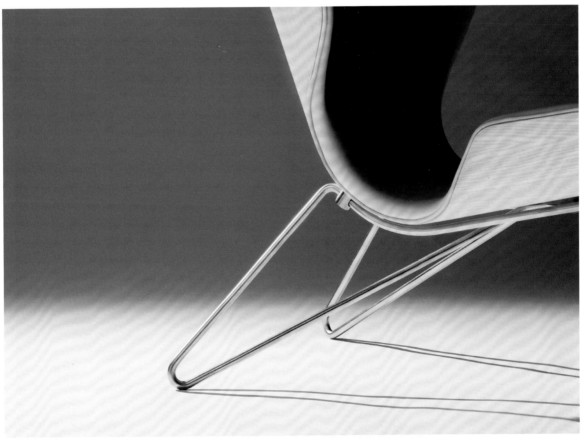

VIRVOITUKSENTIE - LIVING IN NATURE

Living in Nature is the redevelopment plan for a former eldercare facility located only 2 kilometres from central Turku, Finland. Set on the top of a hill among mature pine trees, SNA's design celebrates the existing condition to emphasize nature, well-being, and community. The new multistorey building has a circular footprint, to convey quiet and introspective retreat from fast-paced urban life. SNA also conceived this shape to enclose the transformed elderly home – which is accessible from reverse-terraced openings placed along the building perimeter – and to minimize intrusion on surrounding trees and rock formations.

While the forest introduces a seasonally changing framework for the community to contemplate, highly programmed common spaces encourage interaction between residents. Functions vary from a gym, library, children's room, allotment gardens, and workshops, as well as sauna and spa facilities. These destinations will be installed within the central wing of the former eldercare facility, the renovation of which will reassert its place as the focal point of healthy living. In collaboration with MASU Planning.

The SNA team: Ted Schauman, Jonas Nordgren, Kristian Kontula, Lasse Vejlgård Kristensen, Moritz Schineis, Tymon Wolender, Emanuele Biscaro, Paulina Schroeder, Markus Gustafsson.

HIEDANRANTA INNOVATION BAY

To accommodate 30 percent projected population growth by 2040, the City of Tampere has acquired 250 hectares of waterfront land in its northwest quadrant for 21,000 residents and 8,000 jobs. At the core of the city's investment stand Lielahti Manor and an old factory complex, which have been the source of the Hiedanranta's visual identity to date.

While the urban plan for the neighbourhood underlines the character of the manor and factory, its 30-year vision for this former industrial district will transform the sprawling cityscape into a carbon-neutral live-work hub dedicated to the circular economy. The plan is especially committed to turning Hiedanranta into an urban-scale incubator of new ideas, and the design emphasizes multiple experiences, attractive business environments, and green city planning to attain that end. The masterplan was conceived in collaboration with Mandaworks, Noan Architects, Tupa Architecture, Jolma Architects and Rambøll Finland. The SNA team: Ted Schauman, Jonas Nordgren, Kristian Kontula, Ella Kaira, Jaap van den Hoogen, Ulrik Montnemery, Anna-Sofia Lavanti and Sara Zapotoczna.

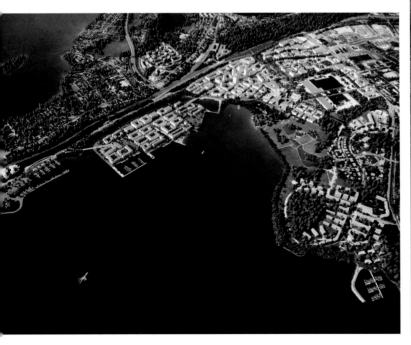

SNORRE STINESSEN ARCHITECTURE

Snorre Stinessen

Stinessen is committed to developing projects that are conscious of our surroundings and the people inhabiting the spaces we create. Interest, respect and curiosity are keywords to our processes. The studio provides a full range of services from architecture to interior and furniture design. We deliver tailor-made projects and products through a close interaction and dedicated service to our clients.

TROMSØ I NORWAY

THE MANSHAUSEN ISLAND RESORT

Manshausen Island is situated in the Steigen Archipelago off the coast of Northern Norway and is home to the world´s largest population of Sea Eagles. The Island´s position between majestic mountains and the Barents Sea is in itself the inspiration for the design. The resort is organized with guestrooms as individual cabins placed at the tip of the rocky formations of the Island, where the positioning in the landscape ensures an immersive, yet private, view to the majestic nature and the elements outside. The shelter design endeavors to make a minimum environmental impact with minimum footprint and the use of cross laminated timber construction. The old farmhouse was renovated and converted to restaurant and library and a sauna was made in the natural pond using left over materials.

EFJORD RETREAT

Efjord is a branch off the Ofoten fiord in northern Norway. The client desired a retreat that focused on the panoramic views of the site, but which also transported them to a feeling of isolation and total privacy, away from hectic work-days in the city. The conceptual layout opens and closes the building in different directions, where the eastern part of the cabin closes towards some neighbouring buildings and opens towards a ridge and the close terrain on the other side. The opposite directions are sought at the front end of the cabin, opening up to the magnificent views towards the dramatic mountains and the fiord to the west. The two volumes are slightly offset to provide for sheltered outdoor areas and views towards the fiord also from the rear volume.

PRIVATE RETREAT

The clients are a family with small children, and also wanted room for the larger family and friends. The conceptual layout was conceived as several individual volumes connected via in-between spaces and a central winter garden, placed on a natural shelf in the terrain. The organisation provides both privacy and room for several activities at the same time. The central winter garden, with fireplace and outdoor kitchen, function as the entrance to the building. From here the retreat opens up to the natural clearing in the forest and from here you enter into either the main building or the annexe. Each group of rooms are done as separate volumes to achieve an additional layer of privacy, but also to emphasize the transition between spaces and activities and tell a story of everyday journeys.

TEGNESTUEN LOKAL

Christopher Carlsen, Morten Bang

Tegnestuen LOKAL is a young design practice, established in 2015 with the explicit aim to create sustainable architecture that respects and develops our Nordic cultural heritage. The goal is to devise and build architecture that supports identity and diversity rather than homogenization in a world that grows smaller day by day. When working with any architectural project, the baseline is always the specific context, its potentials and challenges. Potentials are reinforced and relevant qualities are processed to support future use. Overall, we work with three different subjects that combined create a holistic foundation for the development of the project: Culture, People and Environment.

Culture is about understanding and reinterpreting the local architectural and cultural specificity. We respect and conserve the historical layers so future architecture becomes a natural extension of the traditions that Nordic architecture is conceived within and not a technological statement without root in its context. Nurturing the local cultural specificity supports identity, recognizability and attachment, which generates community and unity.

People are the primary subject of our work with architecture. Our projects are designed for people and the use of our buildings should support a sustainable lifestyle. This is addressed by designing for a high degree of local community. Community is an asset that has been neglected for years, with focus shifting to private ownership but it is slowly resurfacing because of social, environmental and economic advantages. Community breeds security, is practical and ensures better use of resources.

Environment is more important than ever and we work focused on creating architecture that has a positive effect on our local and global environment. We always explore the possibility of producing and handling energy, water and heat locally through renewable sources, but we also focus on the impact of our materials on the global environment.

COPENHAGEN I DENMARK

ØRSTED GARDENS

Ørsted Gardens grew out of an ordinary facade renovation, aimed to prevent water from damaging the concrete balconies, into a drastic alteration of the building's semi-private spaces and a radical reinvention of the facade facing HC Ørstedsvej. To create a new kind of social space, a series of glass bays were added to the architecture, creating semi-private decks for the individual residents. The private balconies are placed on the outside of the access way, which creates a space that is at the same time private and shared encouraging random meetings between residents. The balconies shift story by story generating a lively facade pattern, that introduces rhythm to the street, where before there was none. On top of each bay, a garden crowns the structure, spanning from the inside to the outside and softening the design. On the inside the gardens serve as a bed for growing eatable plants and herbs.

TK-33

The focus of TK-33 is to identify CO2-heavy elements of the typical Danish house and replace them with eco-friendly alternatives in a contemporary formal language that resonates with the existing qualities of the town. Concrete and brick building components of a typical house are replaced by a wooden load-bearing structure, clad in a thin layer of tile shingles, which reduce emissions associated with the outer walls that usually account for 30% of the total emissions during the construction phase. In addition, the facade system is C2C-certified allowing for reuse or gradual replacement and the distribution of the interior spaces allows for natural ventilation and a high degree of flexibility, extending the use of the house across owners. Common areas are organized around the kitchen and expand into the natural landscape, aided by the height of the interior spaces.

AMARYLLIS HOUSE

In their winning proposal for the competition for the first tower in Grønttorvet (the former vegetable market outside Copenhagen), Tegnestuen LOKAL drew inspiration from the area's industrial history to create a landmark with a green identity for the neighborhood. The result is an architectural statement that incorporates private gardens into the apartments of the tower, while, from a distance, signaling the history of the area and the industrial scale. The balconies and gardens are nestled into the structure giving the tower a clear, legible and expressive relief from a distance that scales down as you approach it. A palette of red/brown bricks grounds the building with Copenhagen's history and a special emphasis has been put on detailing the brickwork of the new buildings. The tower and building body integrate the history of the vegetable market with the buildings by creating a vernacular of clear-cut, well-detailed volumes of bricks and plants.

THG ARCHITECTS

Oddur Kr. Finnbjarnarson, Halldór Guðmundsson,
Freyr Frostason, Paolo Gianfrancesco, Elínbjörg Gunnarsdóttir
Ragnar Auðunn Birgisson, Samúel Guðmundsson

THG Architects, founded by Halldór Guðmundsson in October 1994, operates in the fields of architecture, design and project management. The staff holds a varied experience in architecture, design and city planning as well as project management and supervision of building projects, both new and renovation of buildings and institutions. From the start, the company has aimed at fulfill the client's wishes and needs in a professional and practical manner. The firm has been among forerunners in architecture in Iceland and one of THG's specialties is the staff which specializes in project management and supervision.

KLÍNIKIN - THE CLINIC

A privately owned practice of diverse doctor's disciplines and health care practices. It consists of a home base for home care practices, private consulting rooms and three fully equipped operating theatres with recovery and support facilities. The building used to be one of Scandinavia's biggest disco, with multilevel seating arrangement and a stage / dance floor. One of the main challenge in renovating the building was to simplify the levels and create a bright and appealing space as well as to ensure that the flow of patients, staff and goods were clinically accurate despite the old structure being designed around a totally different function and a fully operating hotel on the floors above. The introduction of a big skylight above a double story center, creates an awareness of the exterior and brings daylight down into the core of the operation.

REYKJAVÍK KONSÚLAT HOTEL – CURIO COLLECTION BY HILTON

The project involves THG Architects in all aspects, from urban planning architecture, interior details and management of the construction. Transformation of a listed building, preserved building and a new building is the main goal for the project. The concept has been developed around the historical figure of Consul Ditlev Thomsen, the owner of the great department store Thomsen Magasine, which in 19th Century established a legacy of international hospitality and retail in Iceland. An impression of the old "Coal alley" is imprinted through the lobby on ground floor. The project team has enhanced the timeless charm of the spaces through details, materials, colour palette and iconic furniture. The result is a fluid and permeable space, where clients and locals naturally blend.

BLACK DIAMOND HOUSING AND RETAIL – M. RARGATA 18

A small dark diamond by Reykjavík harbour includes a restaurant and retail on ground floor with apartments on upper floors and a roof top terrace. The building is designed as a floating, dark, skewed cube on top of a heavy, stone pillar. The cladding material is dark zinc with natural stone on ground floor and larch wood in balconies. The apartments are designed in modern, Scandinavian style with fantastic views towards the harbour area. The material palette for the interior is a mix of concrete, wood and dark metal. On the hallways a panoramic scene is presented from an aerial landscape in Iceland which is reflected in the building architecture.

STUDENT HOUSING COMPLEX – BRAUTARHOLT 7

The project is a 1st price competition by THG architects. The building is built around a central courtyard where the students' meeting area is. There are 109 apartments in the house of different sizes and types that are suitable for both individuals and couples. The basement (ground) floor is a mix of gathering spaces, café, laundry room, post office and bicycle storage which open into the courtyard. On the top floor some outdoor collaborative spaces are located for residents to gather. The material is a mix of concrete, corrugated metal and wood. The colour pallet is simple primary colours with simple white and grey tones.

TRIGUEIROS ARCHITECTURE

Vasco Trigueiros, Maria Sigeman Trigueiros

Trigueiros Architecture is an architectural design studio based in Stockholm since 2003. We unite particular skills with a Passion to stretch Creativity beyond the Perception of styles: The Aesthetic is rather the results of experiences and origin. We develop extraordinary and highly innovative architecture, combining contemporary flavors, international ambitions, and a true Scandinavian heritage. We always strive for results and simplicity, using Sensibility, Playfulness and Honesty as value creation basics. We design in high international standard adding values and durability. We work systematically and carefully with our clients and their visions. Each project being completed from sketch to ensuring craftsmanship on site. Assignments include private villas, furniture design, residential areas, commercial space etc. Architect Vasco Trigueiros originates from Brazil & Sweden runs the company with Maria Sigeman Trigueiros. Together with their team of highly dedicated colleges, the experience of projects runs scales from interior design to property development.

VILLA TORÖ

The cliff landscape, minerally ground, organic pine trees and heavy winds gives form to *Villa Torö*. Its positioning at a ridge of the cliff landscape in Stockholm archipelago offers a generous view above the treetops. The barren landscape with colours of light grey and brown is reflected in the building's facade where the materials natural colours are left untouched. Ruff cedar wooden boards contrast the enclosed refined concrete shape. Magical pine trees follow the buildings' confident posture. Its graphic play between shapes and materials creates a dynamic yet monolithic shape and breaks up the large volume into a smaller scale. The materials on the outside continues to the interior. Mineral walls and wooden surfaces interplay throughout the house. Carefully crafted furniture picks up the colours of surroundings becoming one with the framed views. Each room with its own quality in relation to the outside; closeness to the rock, spaces among the treetops, hidden niches and a sunny atrium creating a haven from the harsh winds.

CONE HOUSE

Sloping like the site it sits on the *Cone House* playfully adjusts to its surrounding in the Stockholm archipelago. The building seems to be stretching down towards the water just meters away. The challenges of the modern shape draped in a traditional cedar chip facade is met by great craftsmanship with its carefully executed details. The technic rooted in the traditional wood chip church facades is in this project given a new take. Both expressive yet minimalistic the shape conceals a dynamic interior where ceiling height varies from 2,5 to 7,5 meters. Entering the house, a landscape of spaces on different levels is revealed opening up towards the water. Like a backbone the straight oak stair spans the full length of the house connecting all spaces from the south porch to the north porch. A minimalistic light interior clad with parts in oak wood and Swedish marble creates an honest interior.

245

VILLA LILLVIKEN

Like an erratic block tucked in a crevice of the cliff, the building blends in with its surrounding. The endless force of nature has shaped the rocks creating a sheltered space from the southeast ocean storms. With time it will also drain the colours of the wood giving it the same silvery tones as the surrounding rocks. The changing seasons of the scenery outside is present in every room through the large glass surfaces as well as smaller carefully framed views bringing the nature into the house. The closeness to the raging waves from the inside gives the feeling of being at sea. Inside colours and materials are carefully picked to create a calm entity. Bricks from the north of Sweden, linen textiles and oak wood. Together with the carefully crafted furniture the interior has a strong Scandinavian root with an international touch.

TUOMO SIITONEN ARCHITECTS

Tuomo Siitonen

Tuomo Siitonen Architects are working on a broad range of projects, from town planning to interior design. The company emphasises elegance and ecology in all its architectural solutions, no matter the scale of the projects. Siitonen has received the Finnish State Art Prize for Architecture exceptionally twice. While presenting the award, the jury noted: "His architecture is characterised by a confident and clear allocation of masses supported by the choice of simple materials. The complex buildings have been fashioned in a functionally logical and rational way, and are sited in their environment with a protective sense of location. Including details and interiors, the carefully planned buildings stand for both reason and emotion."

LEPPÄSUO TRIANGLE

"The Leppäsuo Triangle" housing block offers a new interpretation of the closed block typical for the Töölö-area in Helsinki. Intact street facades have traditionally enclosed a diverse courtyard micro cosmos. A new building type with a sloping roof shapes the scale of the court yard space, improves its lighting properties and produces characteristic residential interiors.

STUDIO FOR A CERAMIC ARTIST

During the last 25 years ceramic artist Karin Widnäs has had a studio and residence built for herself in the Fiskars Artesian Village. It has been built using only local materials and making the best possible use of local expertise, renewable resources, and geothermal energy. As of 2020, ceramics museum is also nearing completion. The buildings also serve as a demonstration and test site for handmade building ceramics.

SMOKE SAUNA, ASIKKALA

The idea of a lake shore sauna is spiritual cleansing. Architectural means have been used to make the experience as full as possible by appealing to all senses. The beauty of the Finnish lake landscape, the warmth of the stove, the smell of smoke and tar and the haptic power of the massive log surfaces produce an experience that is crowned by a dip into the cool lake water.

HELSINKI COURT HOUSE, REFURBISHMENT OF AN OLD ALCOHOL FACTORY

The industrial structures of the old alcohol factory exuding metaphysical power and inspiring confidence, were given a central role in the interior of the courthouse and were harnessed to serve the public image of the judiciary. Upon the completion of the renovation, the project was awarded the Concrete Architecture Award of the Year.

VARIOUS ARCHITECTS

Ibrahim Elhayawan, Alexander H. Berg

VARIOUS ARCHITECTS was founded in January 2008 in Oslo, Norway. We design different types and scales of projects, ranging from 200 m² houses to 50,000 m² master planning projects with mix between public and private projects.

DESIGN PROCESS: as the name implies, Various Architects has a collaborative philosophy. Our designs are the product of a collaboration of creative individuals working towards a common goal – great architecture. With diverse backgrounds we enjoy a unique mix of attitudes and inspiration in our work. Together we strive to create engaging architecture which is in line with social development and meet client needs and budgets. Our architecture is the result of innovative design taking into account the environment, the use, people and communities within budgets of the projects. We have a network of architects, artists, landscape architects, interior designers and product designers that we like to involve in our projects where appropriate. Our office space is a creative co-working environment where we share our space with architects, interior architects and colour designers. The synergy of disciplines is a source of inspiration for everyone involved.

SUSTAINABILITY: environmental solutions and innovative sustainable designs have been prioritized in all projects since the establishment of the company. Our Mobile Performance Venue has been hailed by the press for it's lightweight design and 100% recyclable structure. We have collaborated with the Norwegian research institution Bioforsk in the design of an environmental park that would actively clean toxic airport waste at Schiphol Airport with natural plant processes and a bio-gas plant that would turn organic waste into energy.

TECHNOLOGY: including 3D modeling, parametric design, photorealistic rendering and building information models are all everyday tools in use at Various Architects. We use our detailed knowledge of technology where appropriate, and as a means to an end not as an end in itself.

OSLO I NORWAY

LILLESTRØM BICYCLE HOTEL

The design of the building focuses on making a positive contribution to the surroundings. The project gives back to the city the area it takes away by providing a public green rooftop, which directly connects to the main square of the adjacent Train Station.

The concept is to create a dynamic wooden roof resting on a glass box: The box consists of semi transparent glass walls and a playful concrete base that protects the building against heavy traffic. The transparent glass walls allow natural light to filter through during the day and transform the building into a glowing box at night, creating a special visual experience.

The free form wooden roof, slopes diagonally towards the train station plaza. This gesture provides an inviting public access to the top. The roof is conformed by furnishing, vegetation, stairs and slopes, creating a unique experience with a panoramic view towards city. The glass walls continue over the roof, turning into the balustrade around the public area. The roof then penetrates through the walls to frame the entrance and to provide shelter. The interior space focuses on the function of the building with natural surfaces. The bicycle racks become the main element in the space.

LOKOMOTIVSTALLEN

This historical building is located in a locomotive industrial zone in Oslo center. The existing building has distinctive proportions of 205 meters long and 7 meters wide. The project combines historical restoration with contemporary office spaces.

The concept is to create various wooden boxes that intrude through the original brick facade, in order to break the narrow monotony of the building and provide functional spaces. These boxes have different sizes accommodate a variety of functions. A new elevator tower was created to establish universal accessibility. The tower cladded with brick, identical to the original building, establishes a new landmark, with a trademark railway clock on top.

The largest wooden box houses the canteen, which double functions as the central meeting area in the building. The office spaces can be transformed according to the user needs. Micro spaces can be found along the office area. These small rooms are flexible and can be used for phone calls, small meetings, meditation, etc.

The design process focused on recycling and transforming an existing building to give it new functions in order to have a positive environmental impact. The project transformation was hailed by the Cultural Heritage Management for it´s environmental approach.

THE MOBILE PERFORMANCE VENUE

The Venue is designed to represent Arts Alliance Productions worldwide. The projects is to be the largest mobile venue in the world. A dynamic oval form of 90 m by 60 m, ranges from 10 m to 17 m tall. The project is divided into 20 structural segments that can be combined forming various configurations, with a variety of seating alternatives and stages for live performances.

The main goal was to make the structure as lightweight and compact as possible. This is achieved by the self-supporting PVC skin of hexagonal inflated tubes that form the front-of-house and back-of-house spaces. The specified fire resistant PVC fabric is durable and 100% recyclable. An extremely efficient 'bicycle wheel' truss provides lateral stability for the project and full or partial coverage of the performance space. Supported by standard aluminum staging components this structure is also lightweight and recyclable. The public plaza is formed by an arcade of open hexagons at ground level that mark a clear entrance to the otherwise closed form. The central oculus can also be covered with an inflatable cap. The whole structure requires just one week for assembly and is reduced to only 4% of its volume during transportation.

YRKI ARCHITECTS

Ásdís Helga Ágústsdóttir, Sólveig Berg, Sigurður Kolbeinsson,
Yngvi Karl Sigurjónsson, Magnús Már Þorvarðarson,
Daniel Collovich Axelsen, Gunnar Ágústsson,
Melanie Ingeborg Lorenz, Kasper Brunings, Ingibjörg Benediktsdóttir

The name Yrki has more than one meaning in Icelandic. To cultivate. To grow. To compose. The name stands for our aim to unify the earthbound and the poetic by a sensitive approach to the disparate elements of a specific site. Our goal is the clear statement in the urban and natural environment. Founded in 1997, Yrki architects have designed a wide range of projects, focusing on quality and creativity. The firm is in good standing among architectural firms in Iceland, with a diverse portfolio of completed works and works in progress, including a home for physically handicapped people, a freezer storage for a shipping company, a primary school and a museum. Seeking evidence and guidelines on each specific site, we aim at integrating the functional and the visual. We hope that our work is the result of a critical assessment of the environment, showing it the respect it deserves.

REYKJAVÍK | ICELAND

SIX HOUSES AT THE OLD HARBOUR

Located on a wharf in the old harbour of Reykjavik, these six wooden houses were designed to replace a cluster of run-down sheds housing ticket offices for whale watching and sightseeing enterprises. The project is part of an urban planning effort in making the old harbour more attractive for the public as more and more restaurants, shops and other services have settled in this area for the past years. The inspiration for this project was an old photograph showing long gone wooden houses with the gable facing an ancient alley in the vicinity of the old harbour. The wooden houses are linked together by spacious verandas, with seating areas and storage units for marine equipment. The random character of the former sheds is replaced by a disciplined scheme of repetitive structures and designs and a limited choice of materials. The small scale of the houses calls for a careful treatment of each detail.

PATIENT HOTEL

The patient hotel on the premises of the National University Hospital of Iceland was a joint project between Yrki architects and Gláma / Kím architects. Focusing on the exterior, Yrki architects designed the granite and basalt cladding of the facades in collaboration with artist Finnbogi Pétursson. The various sizes of the granite slabs, their rhythmical order and different textures give a unique character to the essential structure of the building. Finnbogi Pétursson is one of Iceland´s most prominent artists, known for his work that fuses sound, light, sculpture, architecture and drawings. On the patient hotel project, entitled Berg, Pétursson writes that it refers to the geological layers of granite that have built Iceland for the past three million years. "Instead of focusing on one part of the building, I wanted to work on a visual interpretation of this natural phenomenon on all the facades". The stone cladding can be read as a work on its own, with a poetic dimension to its minimalist character.

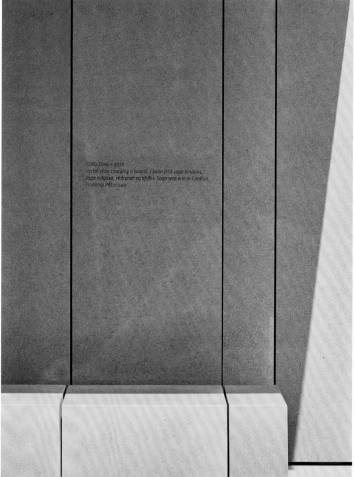

STUDENT HOUSING

The student housing on the campus of the University of Iceland offers 140 apartments for 244 residents. Built around a bright, spacious garden, the western building houses communal apartments and shared facilities, a.o. a garden pavilion with a café and lounge. The one- and two-room apartments for singles and couples are in the eastern building. A maximum use of the allowed building coverage was among the prerequisites of the client. Avoiding a monotonous look, the character of the two buildings of this largest student housing complex in Iceland is distinctive by a choice of various materials, colours and designs. Aluminium cladding in various colours alternates with fair-faced concrete. The three-dimensional structure of the western building is in balanced contrast with the modular order of the facades of the eastern building.

SVEINATUNGA

In 2015, Yrki architects won the 1st prize in an invited competition for the interior design of the new conference facilities for a city council. The facilities host the council´s meetings as well as exhibitions and receptions. Great flexibility and multipurpose-use were among the key factors in the design process. The space can be divided with movable walls into rooms of different sizes. The rooms are easily reconfigured for various purposes such as meetings, exhibitions and receptions. Care for materials and detail were the other key factors in the design process. The wooden panels, with their specific colours and textures, are a core element of the decisive character of the space. The design is thorough to the smallest detail, as we believe that the beauty of any design lies in its details. The project is neither trendy nor fashionable. Its classic aesthetic quality goes hand in hand with its functionality.

ZEPPELIN ARKITEKTAR

Orri Árnason

We cherish the traditional Japanese way of approaching a new project. They apologise to the local spirits for interrupting their peace and promise to do nurture their home. We like to think we are the spirits of our projects. We believe it helps, just like when one is running and thinks he is an agile animal, and therefore runs with more grace. We take neglected sites and imbue them with a sense of magic and wonder by designing something totally unexpected. It is fundamental to us that we form an emotional understanding and connection with the building and its site and nurture this connection throughout its development. Our understanding of the impact on the environment takes a central role in how we develop our schemes where long lasting functionality and flexibility along with connection with the landscape, location and proximate community take priority. Using the latest technology, we develop innovative design proposals that inject a sense of delight into the most practical design briefs for a broad range of clients, from young private individuals to multinational corporations. Drawing on a vast range of experience of the team, Zeppelin Arkitektar is constantly pushing boundaries.

REYKJAVÍK I ICELAND

RÁNARGRUND 4, GARÐABÆ

The restaurant was built in Garðabær following a successful 1 st place in a design competition. Located on a popular coastal bike path, this building connects Reykjavik to the suburb of Garðabær. The restaurant is situated between a school Zeppelin Arkitektar designed several years ago and an open area to be developed into a public space. It was developed as a retreat for cyclists and walkers who travel along the coastal path, and as a place for events and small concerts. The concept was to make a building from where you could admire the sunset and the view of Snæfellsjökull – the glacier which Jules Verne made famous in his story Journey to the centre of the Earth. With large windows, it is orientated to the north west so visitors can comfortably sit sheltered inside and admire the stunning sunsets and views. High ceilings and adaptable spaces with a centrally located kitchen allow the building to be used in different configurations and functions from café to restaurant and event space, both inside and out. Exterior steps flow up the end of the building connecting the south facing sheltered seating area to the roof terrace. The building is made of cross laminated wood elements, walls clad with larch and roofs covered with turf. The building sits as a part of the landscape, and offers a welcome pause for the community and visitors alike.

RIVER LAGOON SPA

Located in a geothermally active area on the famous Golden Circle tourist route in Iceland, the River Lagoon Spa is an exceptional project. Including a 200 room hotel, two hot lagoon/pools, spa restaurant and service centre, it marries nature with luxury. To be built on the banks of Brúará river, Iceland's second longest spring river, the spa benefits from naturally heated water bubbling up from below the earth's crust, making the luxury of unlimited hot water and electricity fully accessible year round with an extremely low carbon footprint. The building is designed to protect the two hot lagoons from cold northern winds, while providing guests with the superb views from their rooms, taking in the northern lights in winter and the river and sun in the summer. The form of the building also draws from the surrounding nature features, nearby green hills standing above the flat land and a necklace of distant mountains. We also took inspiration from the traditional Icelandic turf houses whose walls were made of earth and stone and had turf roofs. Like the turf houses, the building will seamlessly blend into the landscape and be a place of warmth and sanctuary for guests desiring a luxury escape into nature.

ORKA (CO-LIVING)

Meaning Energy in Icelandic, Orka is one of our most ambitious re-use projects to date. Located on the top of a prominent hill to the North East of Reykjavík, it is built around an imposing complex of six steel hot water holding tanks. Standing high above the suburb of Grafarholt on an underused, prominent site, we propose to build a vertical community. This will comprise a mix of apartments, child care facilities, gym, spa, café, restaurant, offices, greenhouses and a sheltered protected central garden, to become the heart of the neighbourhood. The project involves reversing the negative attitude towards the site by locals who live in fear of the high volume of hot water located above them. By adding extra safety features to protect the inhabitants. The Greenhouses and gardens will be heated all year round and provide opportunities for growing vegetables, fruits and tropical plants. The idea is to provide a new heart for the area with a landmark building offering valuable high density housing supported by strong infrastructural public transport links to the city centre. By night the tops of the green houses located above the hot water tanks glow, offering an impressive landmark seen from several kilometers around, equally offering panoramic views of the stunning surrounding countryside from within.

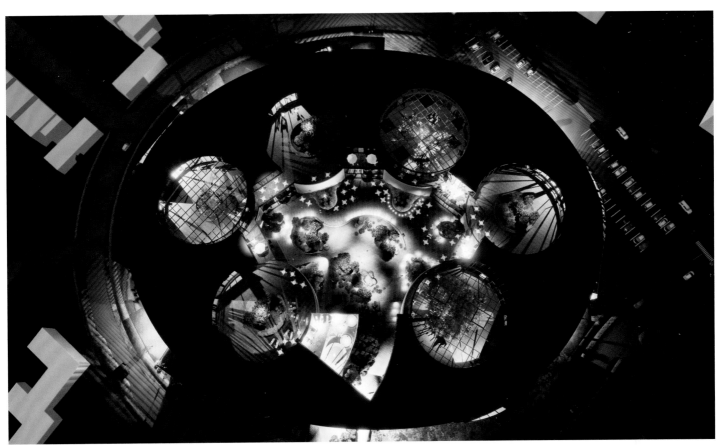

SAILS ON THE POND

Built on a disused industrial site and located in an old industrial part of Akueyri in the North of Iceland, this is a modern collection of residential units, softened by horticultural-architectural features. The area has a rich connection with the history of maritime trading from the 1800s acting as a link between Denmark and Iceland. The black Gránufélags house is located on the site facing the harbour. It was built in several parts in the late 1800s by ambitious Icelanders who challenged the Danish trade monopoly by founding their own trade company called Gránufélagið. It owned four sail ships, Grána, Rósa, Hertha and Njáll which operated from 1869. The four buildings sitting on a single story commercial unit base resemble the sails of the ships and will bear their names. In between the sails, a sheltered green space is provided for residents to grow their own produce. The oldest botanic garden in Iceland was originally created in Akureyri not far from the site. We embraced this history, stepping the blocks back with the gardens growing up the inward facing walls of the scheme from the centre. Far from a new idea, it is one that has been around since the time of the Hanging Gardens of Babylon in 600BC. It was important to us that the building should respect the history and landscape of this beautiful area and a sense of connection with nature, while embracing the need for a large number of housing units.

DIRECTORY

ALT ARKKITEHDIT OY
Hallituskatu 13-17 D, II. krs
FI - 90100 Oulu
T +358 405 959 686
info@alt-arkkitehdit.fi
www.alt-arkkitehdit.fi
Photos: © Ville-Pekka Ikola,
alt ARCHITECTS

ARCASA ARCHITECTS AS
Sagveien 23 C III
NO - 0459 Oslo
T +47 227 170 70
arcasa@arcasa.no
www.arcasa.no
Photos: © Eirik Evjen

ARK-TELLUS AS
Grev Wedels gate 6B
NO - 3111 Tønsberg
T +47 336 970 01
post@ark-tellus.no
www.ark-tellus.no
Photos: © Jan Roger Bodin,
Margaret M. de Lange, Espen Grønli

ARKITEKT MANUELA HARDY AS
Øvrevollen 2
NO - 4319 Sandnes
T +47 978 917 27
manuela@mh-arkitektur.no
www.mh-arkitektur.no
Photos: © Anette Ungar,
Damir Fattakhov

ASAS ARKITEKTUR AS
Grubbegata 14
NO - 0179 Oslo
T +47 917 930 00
asas@as-as.no
www.as-as.no
Photos: © asas arkitektur as,
Fredrik Myhre, Ola Spangen

GOA ARKITEKTKONTOR AS
Nobels gate 35
NO - 0268 Oslo
T +47 224 443 00
M +47 920 800 01
post@goaark.no
www.goaark.no
Photos: © Isaac Voelcker,
GOA Arkitektkontor

GUDMUNDUR JONSSON ARKITEKTKONTOR
Sørkedalsveien 106
NO - 0378 Oslo
M +47 926 492 28
gjonsson@online.no
www.gudmundurjonsson.no
Photos: © Bragi Thor Josefsson,
Jiri Havran

HELIN & CO ARCHITECTS
Urho Kekkosen katu 3B, 3rd floor
FI - 00100 Helsinki
P.O. Box 1333
FI - 00101 Helsinki
T +358 207 577 800
info@helinco.fi
www.helinco.fi
Photos: © Martin Sommerschield,
Mikael Linden, Totti Helin, Marc Goodwin,
Pekka Helin, Antti Laiho, Kuvatoimisto Kuvio,
Jaakko Parkkonen, Tuukka Norri

KAKA ARKITEKTER
Chalmersgatan 1
SE - 41135 Göteborg
T +46 707 202 111
hej@kakaarkitekter.se
www.kakaarkitekter.se
Photos: © Emelie Asplund,
Linda Hutchins, Bert Leandersson

KAMINSKY ARKITEKTUR
Viktor Rydbergsgatan 14
SE - 411 32 Göteborg
T +46 317 612 001
info@kaminsky.se
www.kaminsky.se
Photos: © Kalle Sanner,
Åke E:son Lindman, Mikael Olsson

LARS GITZ ARCHITECTS
Østergade 27, 5. sal
DK - 1100 Copenhagen K.
T +45 333 254 52
lg@larsgitz.dk
www.larsgitz.com
Photos: © Semko Balcerski

LINJA ARKKITEHDIT
Kansankatu 49
FI - 90100 Oulu
T +358 831 137 10
toimisto@linja-arkkitehdit.fi
www.linja-arkkitehdit.fi
Photos: © Imagokuva, Kuvio,
Vesa Voitto Sakari

MAD ARKITEKTER
Nydalsveien 28
NO – 0484 Oslo
T +47 477 525 77
post@mad.no
www.mad.no
Photos: © Kyrre Sundal,
Rasmus Hjortshoj, Jiri Havran

MARGEN WIGOW ARKITEKTKONTOR AB
Fiskargatan 8
SE - 116 20 Stockholm
T +46 739 249 935
cecilia@margenwigow.se
www.margenwigow.se
Photos: © Åke E:son Lidman

NORDIC — OFFICE OF ARCHITECTURE
Kongens gate 21
NO - 0153 Oslo
T +47 229 309 00
info@nordicarch.com
www.nordicarch.com
Photos: © Shiran Photos, Nils Olav Mevatne,
Knut Ramstad, Øyvind Toft, Imarken,
John Arne Bjerknes, Kim Müller,
Nordic – Office of Architecture

PES - ARKKITEHDIT OY
Ison-Antintie 8
FI - 00930 Helsinki
T +358 934 173 40
architects@pesark.com
www.pesark.com
Photos: © Kari Palsila, Marc Goodwin,
Zhewei Shu, Kris Provoost,
Virgile Simon Bertrand

RJ ARKITEKTUR
Kuttervej 15
DK - 9990 Skagen
T +45 312 244 09
rj@rj-arkitektur.dk
www.rj-arkitektur.dk
Photos: © RJ Arkitektur/Rasmus Jørgensen

ROTSTEIN ARKITEKTER AB
Odengatan 85
SE - 113 22 Stockholm
T +46 708 339 270
rickard.rotstein@r2a.se
www.r2a.se
Photos: © Max Plunger, Constantin Meyer,
Åke Lindman, CW Klingspor

SANAKSENAHO ARKKITEHDIT OY
Sepänkatu 15 C 45
FI - 00150 Helsinki
T +358 505 612 495
T +358 505 714 900
ark@sanaksenaho.com
www.kolumbus.fi/sanaksenaho
Photos: © Tuomas Uusheimo, Jussi Tiainen

SCHAUMAN & NORDGREN ARCHITECTS APS
Bragesgade 10B st
DK - 2200 Copenhagen N
T +45 285 519 90

Köydenpunojankatu 2a E2
FI - 00180 Helsinki
T +358 400 410 444

info@schauman-nordgren.com
www.schauman-nordgren.com
Photos: © Nicolas Sedlatchek

SNORRE STINESSEN ARCHITECTURE
Storgata 83b
NO - 9008 Tromsø
T +47 915 809 77
ss@snorrestinessen.com
www.snorrestinessen.com
Photos: © Kjell Ove Storvik, Steve King,
Terje Arntsen, Adrien Giret, Snorre Stinessen

TEGNESTUEN LOKAL
Vesterbrogade 20, 1. th,
DK - 1620 Copenhagen
T +45 268 244 13
morten@tegnestuenlokal.dk
christopher@tegnestuenlokal.dk
www.tegnestuenlokal.dk
Photos: © Hampus Berndtson,
Jan Ove Christensen, Peter Jørgensen,
Kristian Lildholdt Hansen, Tom Jersø,
Kirstine Mengel

THG ARKITEKTAR
Faxafen 9
IS - 108 Reykjavík
T +354 545 160 0
thg@thg.is
www.thg.is
Photos: © THG Arkitektar

TRIGUEIROS ARCHITECTURE
Blekingegatan 46
SE - 116 62 Stockholm
T +46 830 992 5
info@trigueiros.net
www.trigueiros.net
Photos: © Trigueiros Architecure,
Åke E:son Lindman, Sanna Dahlén

TUOMO SIITONEN ARKKITEHTITOIMISTO OY
Veneentekijäntie 12
FI - 00210 Helsinki
T +358 505 673 451
tuomo.siitonen@tsi.fi
www.tsi.fi
Photos: © Jussi Tiainen, Tiia Ettala,
Tuomas Uusheimo, Rauno Träskelin,
Chikako Harada

VARIOUS ARCHITECTS AS
Rosenkrantz´gate 7
NO - 0159 Oslo
T +47 920 408 03
contact@various.no
www.variousarchitects.no
Photos: © Ibrahim Elhayawan,
Dawid Nowak, Noemi Fuentes

YRKI ARKITEKTAR EHF
Mýrargötu 26
IS - 101 Reykjavík
T +354 552 662 9
yrki@yrki.is
www.yrki.is
Photos: © Gunnar Sverrisson,
Nanne Springer

ZEPPELIN ARKITEKTAR
Skeifunni 19
IS - 108 Reykjavík
T +354 553 364 0
zeppelin@zeppelin.is
www.zeppelin.is
Photos: © Elsa Björg Magnúsdóttir,
Ari Magg